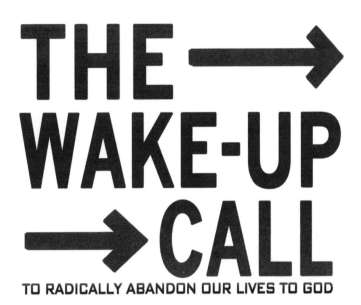

THE WAKE-UP CALL

TO RADICALLY ABANDON OUR LIVES TO GOD

THE →
WAKE-UP
→CALL
TO RADICALLY ABANDON OUR LIVES TO GOD

JOHN MULINDE
WITH MARK DANIEL

Published by World Trumpet Mission
© Copyright 2011 John Mulinde
First printing 2011

ISBN 978-0-615-52777-2

To order additional copies of this book, write to World Trumpet Mission, PO Box 770447, Orlando, FL 32877; email media@worldtrumpet.com; phone (407)846-8300; or order online at www.worldtrumpet.com.

Printed in the United States of America

World Trumpet Mission
PO Box 770447
Orlando, FL 32877
www.worldtrumpet.com

THE → WAKE-UP → CALL

TO RADICALLY ABANDON OUR LIVES TO GOD

Acknowledgment

I thank God, who by his Holy Spirit has given me the privilege to take this journey with him since the day he commanded me over 10 years ago, "Set yourself apart for me. Stay the course and let me do in you the things you cannot do in yourself. You will then be able to help others walk this journey."

It has been an exhilarating journey. The Lord has given me many moments of greatness and has allowed me to see the impact this journey will have. He has opened up to me some very deep things and given me the privilege of glimpsing the possibilities. He has helped me come to believe – and indeed, expect – that whole territories of hardened unbelievers can and will be transformed.

The Lord has accompanied me through some of the greatest trials I have ever experienced. I have learned and continue to learn many lessons. Some of them have been nearly impossible to walk through because they were like strong hurricane winds; they shook and almost uprooted the very foundations of my beliefs. Others stabbed right through the very core of my being until I thought I would probably die because of the numbing grief and disappointment. Yet, God has been faithful to help me stay the course.

The Lord has consistently allowed me to meet and join forces with other men and women who have also begun this same journey of consecration, constantly reminding me that I am not alone. There is always a remnant with whom God divinely connects me, and I am thankful to know that we are on this journey together.

I want to thank
- Pastor Mark Daniel, who gave his heart and time to ensuring the publication of this book. Pastor Mark's heart for the Lord and his Kingdom bless me, and I am very grateful that the Lord joined us together as partners in his work.

- The World Trumpet Mission team in Uganda, who faithfully support me with both their prayers and their friendship. Without this team, not only would this book not be successful, neither would I.
- My wife Sheila and my children, who have made great sacrifices in allowing me to carry the message and the ministry God has given me to the nations. I am thankful for their prayers, love, and support.

I truly treasure these men and women of God who sacrificially give their lives to seeing the purposes of God be fulfilled in our day and time.

Finally, I present this book as a tribute to you, Lord Jesus Christ. You have been faithful and continue to be my covenant friend. You have never left me nor forsaken me. Even when I lost faith, you remained faithful. You have been my refuge, my fortress and strong tower, my very present help in times of trouble, my comforter in deepest grief, and my sun and guiding North Star when all was dark and I was feeling lost and alone. Even when I was walking away from the light, you held me in your grip and caused me to return to my redemptive course time and time again. I call you Faithful. Thank You. I am blessed.

John Mulinde
Kampala, Uganda
2011

Preface

The LORD will guide you always; he will satisfy your needs in a sun-scorched land and will strengthen your frame. You will be like a well-watered garden, like a spring whose waters never fail. Your people will rebuild the ancient ruins and will raise up the age-old foundations; you will be called Repairer of Broken Walls, Restorer of Streets with Dwellings.

Isaiah 58:11-12

This book is based on a continuing journey that I began in 2001 after a life-changing encounter with the Lord. This journey began in Seattle, Washington, on the eve of what has come to be referred to as the 9/11 disaster.

On the evening of September 10, 2001, while in prayer, I was reflecting on the invisible yet powerful "system" which was manifesting itself in various parts of the world and the seemingly insurmountable task of fulfilling the Great Commission as the Church of Christ.

I was asking the Lord several questions:
- What more needs to be done in order for the Church of Christ to have the kind of impact the early Church had, as we read about in the book of Acts?
- What kind of people do we need to be in order to restore the broken foundations in the nations?
- How can we as leaders guide people correctly so they become rebuilders of the broken walls and foundation layers for many generations?
- Is there a strategy to fulfill the Great Commission that was given to us as the Church of Christ?

The Holy Spirit gave me a single answer: "Set yourself apart for me." I did not understand, and he said no more.

The Training Begins

The next day I witnessed the terrorist attacks against the United States on television. We all know what happened: four airplanes hijacked by terrorists were deliberately crashed, killing everyone on board and causing untold carnage. Two of the planes crashed into the Twin Towers of the World Trade Center in New York City, causing them to collapse and killing thousands in the process. One plane crashed into the Pentagon in Washington, DC, killing hundreds, and the fourth plane crashed in a field in Shanksville, PA, after passengers and crew thwarted the hijackers' plans to hit another target, either the White House or the Capital Building.

Such a thing had never been witnessed anywhere in the world. It has proven to be one of the most pivotal moments in the history of the world and has effected the world's security, economy, technology, communications, and every other aspect of world events.

While I was watching televised replays of the terrible tragedy, the Holy Spirit repeated the statement again: "I said, set yourself apart for me," thus beginning the journey of being called to a surrendered life in order to overcome and transform nations. As I have walked this journey, the Lord has continued to unfold his redemptive plan for transforming and discipling the nations through vessels who are set apart for him.

No person or group can deign to fully accomplish the Great Commission single-handedly. Nevertheless, each can be called to fulfill an aspect of this great work. On 9/11, God began to reveal things that touched me deeply. Since then, he has been teaching me that portion which he will have me contribute to the Body of Christ and to the nations at large. I do not claim to have all the answers, but since that time I have taught and shared what he has revealed to me in this and other publications as well as in messages and teachings I have shared in the nations.

The Nazarite Walk

Upon receiving the mandate in 2001 to set myself apart, a few colleagues and I began this journey. We call it "the Nazarite walk." We based this phrase on the biblical term "Nazarite," which is used to describe the vessel who is set apart for God.

As we have walked out this Nazarite journey, we discovered that we are not alone. God has called many others in various nations to this walk. Each of these Nazarites has his or her own unique way of surrendering to God, being set apart to overcome their world, but the principles they are following are all quite similar. This further encouraged me to document what we have learned in our own journey.

It takes a Nazarite – someone totally and radically surrendered to the will and purpose of God – to rebuild the ancient ruins, repair the broken foundations, raise up the age-old foundations, and establish the kingdom of God in their own territory as it is in heaven (Isaiah 58:12). This is who and what the Nazarite walk aspires to make you become.

The Call of the Hour

The call to be set apart for God – to begin your own Nazarite walk – is the call of the hour for the Body of Christ in every nation. This book is the beginning of that journey to a surrendered life. If the Lord has been calling you to surrender yourself to him, and you are ready to set yourself apart, you are reading the right book.

May the Lord who began a good work accomplish it successfully and fully in your life and in mine.

Shalom!

John Mulinde
Kampala, Uganda
2011

Study Leader's Guide

COURSE OVERVIEW:
We have included questions and prayer points at the end of each
chapter of this book so that it can be used as a small-group study.
This is an 18-chapter course divided into 5 sections, and is to help us
see the need to surrender our lives fully to God so that he can use us
to fulfill his purposes in the nations.

It has several purposes:
- To awaken, equip, and provoke the Body of Christ to rise up out
  of its slumber and realign itself with the purposes of God.
- To gain a deeper understanding of how to push back the darkness and to press deeply into the conditions that draw the presence of God.
- To hear the "trumpet call" for a people to be set apart for God in
  deeper levels of surrender and trust, ready and eagerly awaiting
  the coming Day of the Lord.

INSTRUCTIONS TO GROUP LEADER:
We are grateful for your willingness to lead this small group study.
We ask that you would take the role of shepherding your group by
your example of preparedness and prayer. Please commit to being
alert and watchful as you reach out to your group members throughout the week to encourage them to stay the course.

It will be necessary for you to intentionally set aside time each day
to go before the Lord for revelation and insight as well as to stay in
alignment with the heart of God. Know in advance that there will be
spiritual warfare, but that as you stay in your covenant position you
will grow in your faith and learn how to overcome and push back the
resistance of the enemy.

This will be a rewarding and challenging spiritual experience as you determine to plow up the ground of your heart, advancing in deeper levels of surrender and trust with understanding. You will then be able to encourage others in their faith and to humbly lead others in discussion.

As we send out a message that is awakening people out of the flow of the culture and into a lifestyle that begins to seek after God, we have found that being part of a small group of people who are interacting together, praying together, and encouraging each other is vital in helping people maintain progress. Many people are touched at conferences and events, but if they don't get connected with a group of people with the same heart, the sheer force of the culture can begin to pull them back into a less passionate pursuit of God. Therefore, please encourage group members to connect with one another during the week for to pray for, support, and encouragement one another; the group dynamic is vital to seeing awakening spread and deepen.

Finally, as your group completes this book, encourage group members to gather others to lead them through this material. This is a useful tool in awakening God's people, and growing and strengthening his army in your church and community.

INTRODUCTORY MEETING:
You will want to establish a small group that ideally has no more than 10 members. Provide an atmosphere that is prepared in prayer, that is warm and inviting, and where everyone is welcomed and received in love.

Make sure to gather everyone's contact information so you will be able to interact within the group during the week. Communicate this information by e-mail or handout to all group members so they are able to connect with one another during the week. Pass out the *Wake-Up Call* books and collect monies.

Hand out a schedule to help the group members stay consistent and mindful of what lessons you are doing. We recommend that you read at least 2 chapters per week. Encourage everyone to read daily rather than to read all the material in one day; this will help them process the lessons. This book was written to be weightier material, so reading daily will allow the substance of what is being shared to soak into their hearts and give them time to wrestle with it in their spirits.

Encourage group members to take the time to pray daily, using the suggested prayer targets at the end of each chapter to gain ground spiritually.

Format For Introductory Meeting:
1. Have members introduce themselves and briefly state what drew them to the group.
2. Ask for those who are willing to share what God is doing in their lives or how he is moving in their heart.
3. Encourage them to share prayer requests and take the time to pray together and then for each other during the week.

GROUP SESSION FORMAT:
- Ideally you will need 2 hours to spend in discussion and prayer.
- Begin with prayer and worship to prepare the atmosphere for the meeting.
- Pray for the Holy Spirit's leadership and allow him the freedom to direct the session as he wills.
- Overview the chapters.
- Discuss the General Questions at the end of each chapter.
- General Discussion Questions are for the whole group – they allow everyone to discuss the ideas that are being communicated in the chapters
- Break into small groups to discuss the Personal Application Questions at the end of each chapter and to pray for one another.
- Personal Application Questions are for breakout groups – they allow everyone to share and participate, and to share with others what God has been showing and doing in their heart as they go through the book.
- Pray through the practical applications that were discussed during the breakout group time.

COMMITMENT:
Ask each group member to stay the course and commit to the homework and prayer. Ask members to prepare for each meeting by thinking through their answers to the discussion questions at the end of each chapter and being prepared to share. Also encourage the keeping of confidences within the group so that there is an atmosphere of trust and safety, allowing freedom and growth.

Section 1

The State of Our World

Prologue

"From the least to the greatest, all are greedy for gain; prophets and priests alike, all practice deceit. They dress the wound of my people as though it were not serious. 'Peace, peace,' they say, when there is no peace. Are they ashamed of their detestable conduct? No, they have no shame at all; they do not even know how to blush. So they will fall among the fallen; they will be brought down when I punish them," says the LORD. This is what the LORD says: "Stand at the crossroads and look; ask for the ancient paths, ask where the good way is, and walk in it, and you will find rest for your souls. But you said, 'We will not walk in it.' I appointed watchmen over you and said, 'Listen to the sound of the trumpet!' But you said, 'We will not listen.' Therefore hear, you nations; you who are witnesses, observe what will happen to them. Hear, you earth: I am bringing disaster on this people, the fruit of their schemes, because they have not listened to my words and have rejected my law."

Jeremiah 6:13-19

In his Word, the Lord said that because he would tarry in coming, the church would go into slumber. He also said that there would be a midnight call to wake up the Church.

I believe that we are in that end-time season that the Lord spoke of. Darkness can be seen all over the world. There are natural disasters, economic failures, diseases and infirmities, political upheavals, government takeovers, wars, terrorism – one form of disaster after another. Families are shaking. The Church is shaking. The nations are shaking. These waves of devastation keep coming and coming, all over the world, bringing with them fear, panic, perplexity, and confusion.

However, as these shakings come, there is also a wake-up call that is going out. The Lord told us that he would send this wake-up call. He said that he would blow the trumpet and wake up his Bride. He said that there would be a great harvest in the last days and that the glory of the latter house would be greater than the glory of the former house. There will be an end-time revival like the world has never seen or known.

The trumpet is being sounded all across the world. We are seeing God moving across the earth, waking up his people and raising up his army. People in Muslim nations are being awakened in the middle of the night with dreams and revelations of Jesus Christ. The "sleeping giant" of God's church is beginning to rise up in Asia, Indonesia, Egypt, Africa, and parts of the world. People around the world are realizing that God is calling them to abandon themselves to him because he is beginning to raise up a mighty work that he is going to do in the nations, and he is raising up his army to be prepared and dressed and ready for this great move of his Spirit.

Let us not listen, then, to the voices of complacency and lethargy that have kept us from being prepared for the wake-up call. Let us throw off our passive attitudes and begin to allow the Lord to make ready his Bride. Let us shake off the slumber and allow God to raise us up and position us so he can bring forth the end-time harvest and the move of his Spirit that he speaks about in his Word.

Let us listen to the Word and voice of God and seek him for the truth, giving ourselves over to him and allowing him to work in us, to raise us up, and to prepare us for the times that are coming. Let us open our hearts to him so we can hear what the Spirit is saying to the Church, and allow him to use us to wake up those in slumber, to heal the wounded, to open the eyes of the blind, and to set the captives free. Let us take his warnings seriously and determine to believe him, follow after him, and love him with our whole hearts. Let us be prepared to answer the wake-up call that God is issuing out to his Bride.

Chapter 1

Understanding God's Timing and Seasons

From one man he made all the nations, that they should inhabit the whole earth; and he marked out their appointed times in history and the boundaries of their lands. God did this so that they would seek him and perhaps reach out for him and find him, though he is not far from any one of us.

Acts 17:26-27

The God we serve is a God of timings and seasons. He is a God of purpose, and he apportions purpose to what he is doing in each time and season. An important way for us to know how to join God in his work is to understand what he is doing in our season and time.

The Bible always talks about the appointed time or the fullness of time. God is not moving haphazardly or by chance. He has set appointed times. All throughout Scripture you see him referring to this. He would even prepare people for the time, and there would be a window of time for them to respond.

Understanding God's timing and seasons is vital in our walk with him. A large part of what we are going to discuss in this book is the shift that has taken place in the physical and spiritual realms. Understanding what that shift is and how we can respond to it is imperative as the people of God seek to carry out his purposes in our generation.

God Works His Purposes Within His Appointed Time

As the people throughout history and the Bible came to understand and cooperate with what God was doing in a season and the timetable he had set for that season, they began to see God do things that only he can do. It is therefore important that we begin to ask ourselves, "What is God doing in this generation? In this time in history?" Following God's timing is crucial, as evidenced all throughout the Bible. Look at Israel.

In the time of Moses, when the Israelites first arrived at the edge of the Promised Land and the ten spies came back with a negative report, convincing the people to disobey the Lord and not go into the land, God judged them because they missed his timing. The people even tried to go into battle later, but God wouldn't go with them; they had missed his timing (Numbers 14:41-43).

Another example of God doing something in his appointed time is Abraham. God said to him, "I'm going to make a nation out of you, but your descendants will go into exile in another nation. They will stay there 400 years because the sin of the Amorites has not yet reached its full measure. After that, I will come and redeem your descendants and will bring them back to this land I am promising you" (Genesis 12:2-3, 17:3-5, 15:12-16).

A nation was going to be born out of Abraham. There would be a time appointed by God during which this nation would go into captivity. While Abraham's descendants were in exile, the Amorites would continue occupying the land of Canaan, the land God promised to Abraham and his descendants. The Amorites would continue in their wickedness until their sin came to fullness, which, according to God, would take 400 years. After that time, as also appointed by God, Israel would be set free from Egypt and God would bring them back to the land of Canaan. As the Israelites took control of the land of Canaan, they would bring God's judgment on the Amorites.

The Bible says in the book of Galatians 4:45 that in the fullness of time God allowed his Son to come as the Messiah. It was not an accident or a coincidence; it was according to God's timing. When the right time came, God caused it to happen. God had sent a forerunner – John the Baptist – to prepare the way, then Jesus came and brought forth the works of God. Jesus and John the Baptist did these things because it was the timing of the Lord (Matthew 3:15).

Jesus calmly walked through crowds who were threatening to stone him; because he knew it was not the appointed time for him to die, he was not afraid (John 8:59, Luke 4:28-30). Jesus also grieved over Jerusalem because they missed the time of their visitation (Numbers 14:41-43). Jesus lamented for Jerusalem and declared that a time would come when the Temple would be torn down and everything taken away because they missed the timing of the Lord (Luke 19:44). He even predicted, "When you see the armies surrounding Jerusalem then you should know that the time has come. Flee to the mountains"

(Luke 21:20-21). In 70AD, the Romans surrounded Jerusalem and the believers fled to the mountains of Pella (Mark 13:14, Luke 21:20-22). Shortly afterward, the nation of Israel was dispersed throughout the nations of the world. All of this happened in God's appointed timing.

Grace was then opened for the Gentile nations. The Bible talks about the fullness of the Gentiles, that when the fullness of the Gentiles has come, then the door shall be opened again to Israel and the whole remnant shall receive Christ. That is part of the fulfillment we are still waiting to see in God's timing (Romans 11:25-26).

The Lord Reveals His Plans

God and his people have always been involved in world events throughout history. Global and empire alliances have been established, political and social events and changes have taken place, and, in the background, God has been moving and working in his timing.

> Surely the Sovereign LORD does nothing without revealing his plan to his servants the prophets.
> (Amos 3:7)

The Bible says, "Surely the Sovereign LORD does nothing without revealing his plan to his servants the prophets" (Amos 3:7). Throughout time, God has used his prophets to warn about upcoming events. Every time there is a major shift in the world, God speaks to his people and gives them warnings and instructions about what is about to come.

Throughout the Bible, the prophets talked about the time that was coming. They gave warnings about events that were about to happen. They shared with the people ways they needed to prepare themselves for what was coming. They even prophesied words that would be spoken at that time. In God's appointed time and season, every one of the events that was prophesied was fulfilled according to God's plan.

It is important to understand what God is doing across the world in his timing, to recognize what season we are in, what is God doing in the big picture of his purposes, and begin to align our purposes with that. It is so easy sometimes to just be busy doing ministry, but not even have a clue of what God's timing is globally. What is God doing in the world today and how do the pieces he has given to each of us even fit into that? It is crucial to understand God's timing and seasons, and what he is doing in the nations right now.

One example of this is when Israel was exiled to the Babylonian empire. Before Israel was given over to go into exile, God had warned (Jeremiah 25:8-14) through his prophets that it was going to happen. While the Hebrews were in exile, the Lord sent them instructions and gave them his timetable:

> *This is what the LORD Almighty, the God of Israel, says to all those I carried into exile from Jerusalem to Babylon: "Build houses and settle down; plant gardens and eat what they produce. Marry and have sons and daughters; find wives for your sons and give your daughters in marriage, so that they too may have sons and daughters. Increase in number there; do not decrease. Also, seek the peace and prosperity of the city to which I have carried you into exile. Pray to the LORD for it, because if it prospers, you too will prosper...When seventy years are completed for Babylon, I will come to you and fulfill my gracious promise to bring you back to this place.*
>
> Jeremiah 29:4-7,10

When Israel went to Babylon, God spoke to the Israelites and told them to marry, to build houses, and to be prepared to be in exile for a while. They needed to understand what God was doing so they could cooperate with him. His instructions helped guide their prayers, affected even their giftings and how they would be utilized. The season was that Israel was going into exile, but God clearly spoke – to the nation, not just to an individual, a ministry group, or a church – he spoke to the whole nation and began to declare what he was going to do, as well as when and for how long he was going to do it.

Even when the Babylonian empire was about to fall, God moved, warning the people about the major change that was about to come. Remember the writing on the wall (Daniel 5:5-6)? Even before the fall of Babylon to the Medes, God used Daniel to warn Belshazzar of what was about to happen to him and his kingdom. God even spoke to them before

When the time came for the Israelites to return to Israel after they had been exiled in Babylon, God spoke to them. He revealed to them that the time had come, allowing people like Daniel to prepare for the new season through fasting and praying. People may have seen the political changes in the physical realm, but they didn't realize that there were spiritual preparations that needed to be done beforehand.

One political change recorded in history was the fall of the Persian empire to Greece (Daniel 8:1-21). God spoke to Daniel about that change before it happened; the Lord was preparing his people for that major political and social change.

Even with all the prophecies of the coming of the Messiah, few people took the warnings seriously. John the Baptist even came to prepare and make the way for Jesus' coming and people came out into the desert in large groups to be baptized, yet there were few who were ready and prepared for Jesus' coming. They were not looking for the timing of the Lord. They were too busy living their lives, doing their own thing, and going by their own timing and understanding of their little world.

Israel was almost wiped off the map 2,000 years ago. Jesus predicted this event and warned the people to prepare themselves (Luke 21:5-36). God also spoke about the current restoration of the nation of Israel, which began over a half century ago. This political and social event is just now taking place in our time – the whole world is struggling with how to deal with Israel – but spiritually, God had already spoken about these events, giving warnings and instructions for how to prepare for them.

God gave warnings to his people a long time ago, then warned them again when the events were just about to happen. And then they did happen in his appointed time. The world woke up and started to see that they needed to deal with the restoration of Israel; they are still struggling with this up to today.

What Is God Doing Now?
In the next few chapters, we are going to look at what is going on today in the nations and the Church, and even what God has been saying all across the nations. God is clearly speaking; he is speaking to leaders all across the world, he is raising up prayer across the nations like never before. The nations are shaking, the world is shaking in epic proportions, and things have been coming at such a rapid pace the past dozen years. We believe there has been a divine shift taking place in the spiritual realm over the past decade.

God is moving all across this world. It is vital that we stop our "business as usual," all the going about on our own schedule and patterns, and begin to lay everything down and turn our hearts toward the Lord. Begin to even cup our hand to our ear so we can hear his voice. Then we become aware that God is speaking and he wants to say something to us: to his Bride, the Church.

The Lord is speaking about major changes happening around the world. Numerous events – economic, social, political, environmental, spiritual, and so many others – have happened since 9/11, and the world has not been the same. Everything is changing at such a rapid pace, and we need to know what God is saying in this hour so we can prepare and join in with his plans.

What God Has Promised in the Time Ahead

Jesus is coming back for a victorious church, not a defeated church. He said the glory of the latter house shall be greater than the glory of the former house (Haggai 2:9). We are therefore not in a losing battle, brethren; there are yet greater things God is going to do in this world. He promised to rise up; he promised that this Gospel of the kingdom shall be preached in all the world to be a witness to every nation and that then the end shall come (Matthew 24:14). This, too, is in his appointed time.

> Jesus is coming back for a victorious church, not a defeated church. We are therefore not in a losing battle.

Therefore, before the end comes, we can expect a great move of God all over the world. We can expect to see a testimony of God's works in every nation. That is a promise made by Jesus Christ: there will be a witness, a testimony, and evidence of God at work in every nation, and then the end will come.

At times, it may look like the Church is being defeated, but don't go by appearances. Jesus is coming for an overcoming Church, a strong Church, a powerful Church. And I believe that during that appointed time, we will see the greatest harvest of souls that the Church has ever seen in all of history.

Jesus also said that because he would tarry, the Church would fall into slumber, but that there would be a wake-up call that would come in the middle of the night. All across the world, we are seeing the beginnings of that wake-up call happening in the nations. In fact, today there are over 500 communities around the world where transforming revival is taking place.

How Do We Prepare for What God Is Doing in Our Day?

What kind of times are we living in? The times we are living in are very similar to those described by Jesus as the last days:

> *"Teacher," they asked, "when will these things happen? And what will be the sign that they are about to take place?" He replied: "Watch out that you are not deceived. For many will come in my name, claiming, 'I am he,' and, 'The time is near.' Do not follow them. When you hear of wars and uprisings, do not be frightened. These things must happen first, but the end will not come right away." Then he said to them: "Nation will rise against nation, and kingdom against kingdom. There will be great earthquakes, famines and pestilences in various places, and fearful events and great signs from heaven. But before all this, they will seize you and persecute you. They will hand you over to synagogues and put you in prison, and you will be brought before kings and governors, and all on account of my name. And so you will bear testimony to me. But make up your mind not to worry beforehand how you will defend yourselves. For I will give you words and wisdom that none of your adversaries will be able to resist or contradict. You will be betrayed even by parents, brothers and sisters, relatives and friends, and they will put some of you to death. Everyone will hate you because of me. But not a hair of your head will perish. Stand firm, and you will win life. When you see Jerusalem being surrounded by armies, you will know that its desolation is near. Then let those who are in Judea flee to the mountains, let those in the city get out, and let those in the country not enter the city. For this is the time of punishment in fulfillment of all that has been written. How dreadful it will be in those days for pregnant women and nursing mothers! There will be great distress in the land and wrath against this people. They will fall by the sword and will be taken as prisoners to all the nations. Jerusalem will be trampled on by the Gentiles until the times of the Gentiles are fulfilled. There will be signs in the sun, moon and stars. On the earth, nations will be in anguish and perplexity at the roaring and tossing of the sea. People will faint from terror, apprehensive of what is coming on the world, for the heavenly bodies will be shaken."*
>
> Luke 21:7-26

Beloved, according to the Scriptures and to what men and women all over the world are sensing and hearing from the Lord, a mighty move of God is about to sweep across the world. But God does not work alone; he works with humans. And he has dug deep wells all over the world to begin to prepare his people for "such a time as this." As we see all the panic and fear, immorality, perversions, poverty, famines, diseases, devastation – as we see disorder of every kind beginning to spread around the world, into every nation – even as we see worldliness and compromise beginning to creep into the Church and the Church beginning to lose its standing and influence in the culture and the public discourse, we believe that this is evidence that God is bringing about his plans and purposes in his appointed timing.

All across this world, God is raising up a remnant. He is issuing a wake-up call and raising up an alarm; his remnant is rising up. We believe that a mighty move of God is going to be taking place and, in fact, is already taking place.

> If we are going to rise up to the need of the hour and prepare ourselves for the move of God, we need to know what to do, how to do it, and how to position ourselves.

God is raising up an army. There are people throughout the world who never dreamed that they would be a part of what is happening right now. This may include you. You were not looking for it. You did not desire it. You were not even trying to find it, but it found you. It got hold of you and suddenly you can't stop. Deep, deep inside you know that the hand of the Lord is on you, that God is drawing you. He is preparing you, enabling you to stand.

The key question then is, "How do we prepare for what God is doing in our day?"
- What must we do to begin to see a mighty move of God's Spirit in our lives, in the church, in our cities, and in the nations of the world?
- What kind of mindset should we have?
- What kind of preparations do we need to put in place?
- How do we need to position ourselves?
- What should be the expectations of our labors?

If we are going to rise up to the need of the hour and prepare ourselves for the move of God, we need to know what to do, how to do it, and how to position ourselves. This is what we will be discussing and laying out in the following chapters.

What Must We Do?

To begin to prepare yourself for what the Lord will reveal to you throughout this book, humble yourself and ask, "Lord, what would you have me do?" What must we do to do the works God requires and to join him in his work in this appointed time? This is the cry of our hearts:

- What must we do to do what you require of us, Lord?
- What do you want us to do at such a time as this, Lord?

I invite you to make this your prayer as you prepare to read on:

> "Lord, open my understanding. Speak to me and reveal things to me that I don't now see. What must I do that I may do the works that you require in this time? Father God, even as I come before you, I pray for a heart of brokenness, for humility and sensitivity, and for submission to your Spirit. Amen."

GROUP DISCUSSION QUESTIONS

General Discussion Questions (for the whole group):

1. What is the general teaching we are seeking to grasp in this chapter?
2. What changes do we/you need to make in response to the lesson this week (in actions, mindset, etc)?
3. What conditions do you see in the world today that indicate the nations are being shaken?
4. What are some of the solutions being offered by man? Have they been effective?
5. Do you believe the Church is being effective in the nations? What would you describe as the condition of the Church?
6. Describe the condition of the Church that the Lord is expecting to come back for in Ephesians 5:27. How does it compare to what you are observing today?

Personal Application Questions (for breakout groups):
1. What did the Lord impress upon your heart as you read this week?
2. How do we prepare for what God is doing in our day? What is He calling you to do specifically?
3. How can we pray for one another so we are able to say, "Yes, Lord"?

Weekly Prayer Targets:
1. Pray for the Lord to open and increase your understanding.
2. Pray for a heart of brokenness, humility, repentance, and submission to Him.
3. Ask God to stir in your heart a desire to be in a state of readiness as you wait for his return.

Chapter 2

The State of the Nations

*In the L*ORD *I take refuge. How then can you say to me: "Flee like a bird to your mountain. For look, the wicked bend their bows; they set their arrows against the strings to shoot from the shadows at the upright in heart. When the foundations are being destroyed, what can the righteous do?"*

Psalm 11:1-3

God is always at work. He has different times and different seasons in which he has different plans and goals to accomplish, but they are always at his appointed time and designed to fulfill his redemptive plan. God was fulfilling his plan during Noah's time and in Moses' time; even at the time of the first Church, he was accomplishing his goals among the people. The question therefore arises: What is God doing in our time? To answer this question, we will begin to look at what is taking place in the nations around us and then at the state of the Church.

Jesus said that pestilence, earthquakes, wars, and all kinds of shakings would come in the last days (Matthew 24:7, Mark 13:7-8, Luke 21:9-26). The earth will groan and darkness will suffocate life. Today, nations all over the world are experiencing the effects of darkness, which oppresses, torments, and suppresses.

> There is a world system that is opposed to the purposes of God and the ways of God, and there is a war raging over the nations.

I believe we are in that season of time the Bible describes as the Last Days. The things that are happening in the world – the political turmoil, human reasoning, self-love, natural disasters, and many other things – suggest we are in the times prophesied in the Bible. We are experiencing the kinds of things the Bible said would be happening. I don't know if that season is going to last 10 years, 50 years, it could be more or less, but I believe there are people alive today who will see the unfolding of Scripture as described in the Bible.

The World We Live in Today

The world we are living in today is far from the one that God desired for us, as we can see in Scripture. Around the globe, not only are we experiencing the ravages of earthly nature, we are experiencing the violence of human nature.

We are living in times of devastating natural disasters: earthquakes, tsunamis, hurricanes, volcanoes, floods, mudslides, wildfires, heat waves, and other acts of nature. These are happening all over the world and the aftermath is leaving people destitute and homeless, wrecking the economies of whole nations. The effects are felt all over the world, and are expected to keep affecting the nations for years after they occur.

We are also living in times of genocide, terrorism, gang and tribal warfare, nuclear weapons, corruption, abortion, perversion, occultism, poverty, starvation, disease, humanism, and human reasoning, among so many other forms of violence and evil that are evident worldwide. These, too, leave people in a wake of pain and suffering, creating a sense of hopelessness and despair.

These events are happening so quickly that we don't have time to recover from one crisis before another arises. Things are starting to come at us so fast that we are almost numb to the world around us. And it seems like there is no end in sight.

Sin, the pulls and ways of the world, and darkness are flooding in all over the earth. They are tearing apart relationships and destroying institutions that God has ordained as holy.

Families are being destroyed, marriages are crumbling, children are being pulled into rebellion and selfishness, and people are pursuing "happiness" as they focus on their own individual rights. These and other self-indulgences are increasing and building and spreading to all nations across the world.

Beloved, all of this is the power of evil penetrating human minds and human hearts, destroying the foundations God has given us, the institutions of life that we live by. And this flood of darkness has also weakened the Body of Christ, which is to be the light of the world and bring hope to the nations.

The Web of Deceit We Have Been Drawn Into

When the Moravians took the gospel to the ends of the earth in the early 1700s, they went to America, South America, Africa, and Asia. Europe became the center of Christianity, and for many years Europe and America became the cradle of the Christian faith, sending out missionaries to all the nations of the earth.

In the late 1800s and early 1900s, missionaries from Britain carried out the most effective evangelistic campaigns all over the world. People in Africa and other countries have exalted Britain, Europe, and other Western nations as mission-sending nations who brought the Gospel and development to their continents and nations. They brought about a lot of positive change to Africa, and to other cultures and nations all over the world.

Men and women from these and other Christian nations laid down their lives and labored in ungodly, pagan communities and nations so people could be delivered from the powers of darkness and their animistic, spiritual idolatry. They labored to bring an understanding of Scripture and glory to God, who had changed their own lives and nations during the many waves of revival.

Where Are These Christian Nations Now?

These nations once carried the Gospel all across the world. They helped spread revivals and awakenings all over the earth. What is going on with those nations today? There has been a shift, a change. They have succumbed in so many ways to the behavior and thinking patterns of the world in which we live. The Christian world of Europe and America, which has been quickly becoming more worldly instead of godly, is increasingly turning away from its Biblical foundations and in some cases has turned totally against God and his ways.

There was a time when the Gospel coming from these nations was the most powerful thing touching the whole world, but now instead of turning the nations upside down with the Gospel and missionaries, it is this secular, humanistic, and immoral wave of things such as pornography, divorce, homosexuality, abortion, selfishness, and humanism that is coming out of these nations and flooding the whole world.

The Western world is still very influential spiritually, but the question is, "What kind of influence is it exerting?" Instead of touching the world with missionaries, many of these once-Christian nations are now exporting their worldly values:. Many call themselves "post-Christian" and no longer hold up the Word of God or his ways as important, divine, or sacred.

The spiritual values that are being promoted today are a mixture, and churches all over the world are changing their values, changing their spiritual boundaries, compromising their godly standards, and following the trends and decay that is happening in the culture around them.

The homosexual lifestyle, abortion, and all kinds of abominations that the Bible condemns are today being woven into our theologies and exported as acceptable, modern theologies. It is becoming increasingly harder to stand for Biblical truth than to stand for the compromised theology that is being developed today in the Church. What the Bible calls sin is abounding and wickedness is on the increase. Good is being called evil and evil is being called good (Isaiah 5:20). The Church is increasingly losing its influence over culture and society.

How did it come about that nations, which yesterday were promoters of biblical values and bearers of the light of Jesus Christ, are today promoters of these unbiblical activities around the world? Have the beliefs, zeal, and sacrifice of the early missionaries been in vain?

A few years ago, I had opportunity to visit the House of Commons and the House of Lords in Britain. God showed me that in the past, his Word had been exalted and held in high esteem in Britain. As Parliament was being built, the roofs, walls, and floors were inscribed with the Word of God as a permanent testimony to generations to come that God is the guiding center of all parts of English society.

This is also true of government buildings in the United States, such as the White House, Capital Building, and Supreme Court. The founders of these great civilizations understood that God had a say in all institutions of men. Sadly, though, the only evidence today of yesterday's faith and honor of the Most High God is in the concrete and not in the practices of the people.

Looking For Answers

When and how did the nations get caught in this web of darkness and deceit? How did we come to the point where nations that once took God's Word to the four corners of the earth are now themselves becoming a threat to the very freedom of the Gospel itself?

And in many countries, especially in the traditional Christian world, the Church – which is supposed to bring hope and Christ to the nations – is being marginalized. The Church is increasingly becoming irrelevant and its spiritual voice is increasingly being pushed out of public affairs. In America, the Ten Commandments and prayer have been pushed out of schools and public offices. The judiciary system, which once relied on the Ten Commandments to create laws and public policy, has rejected them.

The push of the world is growing so strong that we are beginning to take on the patterns of the world instead of clinging to the Scriptures and following the ways of God, the mind of God, and the wisdom of God. We are even seeing the ways of the world growing stronger and stronger in the Church.

For example, within the last 10 to 15 years, within the Anglican and Episcopal global communities, there has been talk of ordaining homosexuals as clergy and allowing same-sex couples to marry openly in the church. Having difficulty getting the Latin American and African Church to accept these practices, the Anglican community began to exert a great deal of pressure on delegations from these areas. The Anglicans even tried economic pressure, offers of better positions, and other means to make the Africans and Latin Americans compromise on these points, but the African and South American leaders stood their ground and did not compromise their standards.

This is only the beginning of the pressure that we are going to see and experience. Many Western nations are already putting similar pressures on other less-developed nations, threatening to withhold financial and humanitarian aide if they do not conform to the West's standards of marriage, abortion, and other things that go against traditional biblical principles. This tide continues to increase day by day.

The State of the Nations Is Changing Quickly

The speed and frequency at which these things are happening – the speed at which things are changing and the foundations are crumbling – are mind-boggling. We don't have enough time to deal with one crisis before another hits us. While the world is still trying to raise support for one devastating event, another comes up. We quickly forget what has happened as we become consumed by what happens next. And many people are increasingly caught in those situations of total destruction because there isn't enough time or resources to help them.

Lives are being devastated all over the world. Earthquakes and tsunamis have come so fast on the heels of each other that we even forget what happened yesterday. We hear of floods and mudslides, famines and hunger, terrorism and fear. We are living in a day of political turmoil. We hear of nations that are rocking; their political structures are falling apart and their populations are rising up in rebellion.

We are living in times of global financial crises, when the need for water and food are becoming a daily issue. The price of food and water is going higher and higher, and scientists are telling us that future wars are going to be fought around these commodities. The future that is being predicted is so bleak. We are living in a world in which the shakings are escalating and seem to just climax together into a world that spells failure.

The nations are groaning for hope. The nations are groaning in pain. Even those nations that have resources have been hit by one crisis after another. Look at America. How many natural and other calamities have struck America just this past year? Oil spills, wildfires, floods, tornados, heat waves, draughts, and economic failures. Each one of them is being described as unprecedented and epic in proportion, but they are happening so fast.

Look at what has recently happened in China, Japan, New Zealand, Haiti, and Africa. Add to this the wars and unrest that are taking place all across the Middle East and in so many other countries: Pakistan, Afghanistan, Syria, Libya, Somalia, Yemen, and others. Political unrest and acts or threats of terrorism are touching our lives worldwide on a daily basis. Crime and violence – such as the drug wars in Mexico and the explosion and mass shooting that just occurred in Norway – are increasing and becoming almost daily events. The devastation is all over and is happening so fast that our minds are racing to adapt.

The moral decay we see moving all over the world is growing so fast that you cannot keep the changing values and standards from another part of the world away from your own people. Right now there is a phenomenon called the "emerging global youth culture." The youth of the world are beginning to think alike because of the global village created by ease of communications and idea exchange that is made possible through the internet and access to media. It doesn't matter whether they live in America or in Africa, the youth all over the world are increasingly being exposed to the same ideas, values, and images. No matter where they are from, they have the same aspirations and desires in life. They follow the same celebrities and have the same political views. With the development of online social network devices, such as Facebook and Twitter, they live in another world. They can "romp" all over the globe, sharing views and thoughts, following celebrities and stars. These role models are shaping the values of our youth, who are living beyond their local cultures and becoming increasingly beyond the reach of their parents. Because of this phenomenon, new social values are sweeping across the entire world, and most are not biblical or godly.

These new values and ideas – this moral decay – is coming in like a flood. There is no way to stop it or even slow it down. It is becoming increasingly difficult to limit our children and families, even our own minds, from being exposed to this corruption because it is coming from so many different devices and sources. It is inundating our families, affecting our hearts, causing more and more people to become isolated and numbed from the things of God. We are losing our ability to withstand the force of this flood that is coming.

The influence of media and the internet, the flood of this moral decay, and its acceptance by today's youth is massive and strong. Conscientious parents trying to guide their youth, couples trying to raise up their families, and even Christians trying to walk in the ways of God are finding so much coming at them that it is difficult to hold things together in the sheer force of the pressure that is coming at us.

This is the world we are living in, but where is the Church?

Where Does Our Hope Come From?
The Church is to be the hope of the nations. It is to be showing to the world that there is hope and that the answer is found in Christ. We are to be showing the world that Christ can push back the flood of darkness; he can restore sanity to our lives and to the ways in which

we go about life. The Church is to reveal that God has the power to redeem, deliver, and transform every aspect of our culture and our society, even in the drastic times in which we live. But where is the Church?

> The Church is to be pointing out to the world that there is hope and that the answer is found in Christ.

We are living in difficult times. The communities and nations in which the Church exists are starting to come against traditional biblical beliefs. Things that are displeasing to God are being forced into the Church by government policies and laws that legalize them. There is a social pressure and intimidation that is trying to force the church to succumb to the values and mindsets of this day and time instead of the values and wisdom of God.

Politicians and media personalities today are increasingly encroaching on the moral arena that churches previously held. These people set standards on issues of morality apart from the Church. Those who speak against these changing standards are called haters, bigots, prejudiced, old-fashioned, or abusers of human rights. These human standards dilute God's absolute moral standards. They turn good into "evil" and evil into "good." They bring about compromise in the name of "acceptance." They turn what was considered shameful yesterday into normal behavior today.

When these unbiblical changes started to rear their ugly heads some years ago, the Church quietly retreated into its four walls. Today, however, the Church's doors are being pushed open by laws and belief systems that go against the teachings of the Bible. The Word of God is increasingly being pushed out of schools and public arenas. In some nations, speaking or writing anything that disagrees with the ways of the world system has become a "hate crime" punishable by law. The Church is being forced to bow to the evil demands of this world system or lose its followers, general support, and charitable status, on which it heavily depends.

The Church has begun to fall under the influence, compromise, and world's ways and systems. When we understand the extraordinary pressure that is coming at lives and families in society now and you look at the weakened state of the church, you realize that if it does not rise up, the is no one to lead us out of this chaos and deception that is swirling around the nations.

Conclusion

I am not attempting to offer a simple explanation of how the nations came to be in such turbulent shape. We do need to recognize, however, that there is a world system that is opposed to the purposes of God and the ways of God, and that there is a war raging over the nations.

> God is waking up his Bride, the Church – for this very hour – to rise up and be able to impact the nations.

God gave the Church to the nations as a means of hope. The Church is to be God's redemptive arm to the nations. God has commissioned us to go disciple the nations, but sadly, at this time in history, the Church does not have the impact on the nations it is supposed to have. In fact, in many parts of the world, the Church has been so diminished and its impact on society has become so minimal that it is even being treated by some nations as irrelevant to the current problems and crises they face.

The Bible is clear, however:
- We are the light of the world.
- We are the salt of the earth.
- We are more than conquerors through Christ Jesus, our Lord.
- The one who is in us is greater than the one who is in the world.

> Jesus Christ is coming back for a victorious Church and I believe that in this season and time, God is waking up his Bride, the Church – for this very hour – to rise up and be able to impact the nations.

This is the season in time in which God is going to bring about a mighty movement of his Spirit in his people all across the nations of the world. This has already started. The wake-up call has already begun to go out. We must answer that call, surrender our lives to God, and allow him to awaken us and use us in these times. To help us start that journey, let us begin to honestly look at the state the Church is in today.

GROUP DISCUSSION QUESTIONS

Study Discussion Questions (for the whole group):
1. What is the general teaching we are seeking to grasp in this chapter?
2. What changes do we/you need to make in response to the lesson this week (in actions, mindset, etc)?
3. How would you describe the effects of darkness over the nations today?
4. How have the Western nations strayed from Christianity by turning from their biblical foundations? What kind of influence are they exerting?
5. Give some examples that you see today where good is being called evil and evil is being called good.
6. How do you see the voice of the Church increasingly being pushed out of public affairs?
7. How has the "emerging global youth culture" affected our children, homes, and the Church?

Personal Application Questions (for breakout groups)
1. What did the Lord impress upon your heart as you read this week?
2. Are you finding it increasingly difficult to protect your hearts and mind in fully following God in today's culture? What are some of the challenges you are facing?
3. When you see all that is coming against us, do you find yourself accepting it or resisting it? If so, in what ways? What ways are you doing a little of both?
4. How can we pray for one another as we respond to what God is showing us?

Weekly Prayer Targets:
1. Pray that God with give you the eyes of faith to see beyond what we are experiencing today.
2. Cry out to God for his people to return to him and his ways so he can do a deep work in the hearts of those who are in full surrender and trust.
3. Pray that the Church would hear the call to awaken, resist the ways of the world, and arise in faith to be more than conquerors in Jesus Christ.

Chapter 3

The State of the Church

The bridegroom was a long time in coming, and they all became drowsy and fell asleep. At midnight the cry rang out: 'Here's the bridegroom! Come out to meet him!' Then all the virgins woke up and trimmed their lamps. The foolish ones said to the wise, 'Give us some of your oil; our lamps are going out.' 'No,' they replied, 'there may not be enough for both us and you. Instead, go to those who sell oil and buy some for yourselves.' But while they were on their way to buy the oil, the bridegroom arrived. The virgins who were ready went in with him to the wedding banquet. And the door was shut. Later the others also came. 'Sir! Sir!' they said. 'Open the door for us!' But he replied, 'I tell you the truth, I don't know you.' Therefore keep watch, because you do not know the day or the hour."

Matthew 25:1-13

For us to understand the state of the Church, we need to understand the purposes of God. We need to understand what God has been purposing since the beginning of time and how that began to give context for when God called the church.

As we understand the context through which God is working, we will begin to see clearly what God's desired end for the church is and where we are in those purposes.

Creation

In the beginning, when God saw that all was good, his purpose and plan for Creation was that it would glorify him; that God's glory would be revealed through all of Creation. God made man to commune with him, and gave him authority to rule over everything he had created. But man fell; instead of being dependent and surrendered to God, he began to live according to his own human thinking and corrupt ways.

After the fall of man, it was only a few generations before the people had become wicked and far from God's intended purposes. God saw "that every inclination of the thoughts of [man's] heart was only evil all the time" (Genesis 6:5). Man was not exalting or communing with God; Creation was not glorifying him. Instead, there was corruption in every aspect of society. God grieved that he had made mankind and decided to cleanse the earth of all Creation and start anew with one righteous man: Noah (Genesis 6:6-8).

After the flood, even though God had wiped the earth clean of all Creation and started afresh, he had vowed to never again destroy mankind or the earth because he was pleased with Noah's sacrifice, and he recognized that "every inclination of [man's] heart is evil from childhood" (Genesis 8:20-22), God continued to be about his work. He maintained his focus on the redemption of mankind, and began to raise up nations, with the intention that they would seek him, reach out to him, and find him.

Nations
The nations did not know who God was anymore; they had lost their understanding of their Creator. They became spiritually blind, immoral, and violent. They began to worship the sun and the moon. They worshiped false gods and idols they had created with their own hands.

There began to be great immorality in the nations. Their belief systems, families, and governments weren't serving the people as God intended; they were just serving themselves. They lost perspective of God and his ways, becoming more and more corrupt and getting further and further from God's heart desires.

God had made a vow that he would not destroy mankind again, so he began to work his plan of redemption. What was that plan? To raise up a nation through which he could reveal himself to all the other nations and draw them back to himself; a nation that would reach and impact the other nations of the world.

Although he had rejected the nations because they had departed from him and his ways, God's heart burned for them. The nations had become locked in bondage and corruption, but God's desire was to restore them to himself. They had become so far off track that just one act could not turn them around. They needed to see a nation that was fully given over to God, a nation that depended on him, and through which he could show his character, his love, his power, his provision, and his mercy.

This nation was Israel.

Israel

God had a purpose and a plan: he wanted to raise up a nation through which he could impact all the nations of the world. His desire was to raise up this nation in his ways, his character, and his presence so the nations would see that there is no other God but the God of Israel. He wanted the nations to see the One True God and recognize his power, his glory, his righteousness, and his ways so that they, too, would begin to know him and follow him.

God set the nation of Israel apart and taught them his ways. He gave them instructions and commandments that would make them different from the other nations. His presence was always with them; he led them through the wilderness in a cloud by day and a pillar of fire by night. He fought their battles; he provided for their needs. He watched over them and protected them. All throughout Scripture we see God revealing himself in such a way that the nations recognized that there is no God like the God of Israel (1 Kings 8:23, 2 Kings 18:5, 2 Chronicles 6:14).

> When Israel remained in the position of being set apart to God, God used them to impact the nations, but when Israel began to become like the nations, then the nations began to dominate and overpower them.

Over time, Israel would lose sight of God and would begin to follow the ways of the nations that God had rejected. God had told them not to yoke themselves with other nations, not to marry into them, not to take on their ways and customs. God wanted Israel to be different from the other nations; he wanted Israel to be set apart unto himself so that through them he could reveal himself to the world. When Israel remained in the position of being set apart to God, God used them to impact the nations, but when Israel began to become like the nations, then the nations began to dominate and overpower them.

Whenever Israel would begin to follow the ways of the nations, God would come to Israel and show himself mighty and holy; he would do this in such a way that the people would tremble. And the nations who were watching, who were seeing that there was no god like the God of Israel, would tremble, too.

This is very similar to what is happening in the Church today. The Church is not to be like the world; we are to be set apart unto God. When we are set apart, we impact the world, but when the Church starts to become like the world, then the world begins to dominate and rule over the Church.

During the times that Israel fell away from God and his ways, the people would still be going to the temple. They would still be going through all their feasts and rituals, but they would also be completely off course from the mission God gave them. The Scriptures show that God would warn them over and over again. Sadly, he would sometimes do what he had said and exile them into the very nations they wanted to be like. God would do this to discipline them so they would come back, repent, and choose to walk out the mandate he had given them.

Finally, God began to send prophets to Israel to tell them, "You have lost sight of the mandate God gave you to do, so God is going to send a Suffering Servant, a Savior (Isaiah 42:1-7). He is going to send a Messiah who is going to redeem the nations."

God's redemptive plan was to send a Redeemer – the Messiah – through Israel. The Savior would come to his people himself to work his plan of salvation (Isaiah 59), and out of Israel, all the nations of the world would be blessed, as God had promised Abraham (Genesis 22:17-18). Out of Israel, God would say to the nations, "Come to me, all you who are weary and burdened, and I will give you rest" (Matthew 11:28).

Jesus Christ, the Messiah

Jesus came to earth on a mission that he never strayed from: he called forth the Church and sent them out to disciple the nations and draw people back to communion with God, fulfilling the purposes of God.

Jesus was completely submitted to the Father's plan of redemption to reach the nations. His life was a life of complete mission. He was not here to serve himself, to acquire money or fame, to have a ministry or teaching opportunities. He was here to fulfill his Father's mission. Even when the people wanted to keep him in one place, to make him their leader, he would say, "No, I must be about my Father's business" (Luke 2:49-50, NKJV).

Jesus came to give his life so that the nations could be redeemed and brought back to God. One of the final acts he did was to call forth the Church. He called the Church to go forth and fulfill the Father's mission to impact the nations. He sent them out to reach the nations and to make disciples of all nations.

> *"Go and make disciples of all nations, baptizing them in the name of the Father and of the Son and of the Holy Spirit, and teaching them to obey everything I have commanded you."*
>
> Matthew 28:19-20

Who are we, the Church of Christ, supposed to disciple? The nations. Who are we supposed to be reaching? The nations.

We see the way the nations have veered off course. We see the way the nations are shaking. But Jesus gave the Church a mission. We are to reach and impact the nations. We are to disciple every nation. Scripture says there will be a witness in every nation and then the end will come Matthew 24:14).

The Church

Jesus gave us everything we need – the instructions and keys, gifts and promises, position and authority – to fulfill the Great Commission and to be his agent of redemption to the nations (John 14:12).

Instructions and Keys. Through his death and resurrection, Jesus gave us the way we could walk out the fullness of the life and power that he has given us. He gave us keys that unlock the door so we can go forth in victory and abundance, and be able to accomplish the mission he has called us to.

He told us that we must abide in him, we must cling to him, that we can nothing apart from him. He told us that if we try to do anything in our own power or our own wisdom, we would be able to accomplish nothing. He told us that he is the vine; that all life flows through him and he flows that life in us and it will bear much fruit. It cannot fail but to bring forth fruit. Jesus also told us that we must walk in communion with him (John 15:4-5).

A key to abiding, where our focus, love, and hearts are given over totally to the Lord and where we are walking and living in faith, is believing that God is who he says he is and that we are who he says we are. We must fight the fight of faith to hold onto that belief and not yield it to our enemy. The indwelling presence of the Holy Spirit, who is always with us to guide, counsel, and provide for our every need, is another key to abiding. He provides the flow of life; it is not our life being lived through him, but God's life living through us. When we really learn to abide, a life flows through us that is not our own.

Jesus also told us that we must love him above all other things; he said that this is the most important and greatest thing. It must become the focal point of our life: we are to love God with all of our heart, mind, soul, and strength (Mark 12: 30-31, Luke 10:27). Jesus told us not to love the world. If we love the world, then that love from the Father will dry up in our hearts (1 John 2:15). If we love the world, then we are at enmity with God; we are provoking him to jealousy (James 4:4-5). We must not go after what the world goes after; we are to seek after the Lord and give ourselves – our greatest affection and deepest love – to him. Jesus told us that we are to love each other as he loved us (John 15:12). Love is to be our distinctive; it is the way the world will know that we are his. We walk in that love because we are one body, one Bride, and have one faith. When we really grasp that Jesus holds the greatest affection, that there is no idol or love that usurps him, when we really take hold and give Jesus the fullness of that love, he hands us a key that begins to unlock the things of God.

The enemy wants to compel us to devour each other so that we are wounded and divided, disunified and torn apart (John 10:10), but Jesus told us that we must love each other the way he loved us (John 15:12). He even painted the picture for us with the Good Samaritan (Luke 10:30-37), of washing each other's feet (John 13:4-15), the way that he showed love to the broken and forgotten of society. The way we walk in the law of love is a key. As we love one another the way that Christ loved us – with generosity, sacrifice, and abundance of love – we will make an impact on those around us. Jesus said that we are to love each other in that way, and that by doing that – by loving each other the way that he loved us – the world would know that we are his (John 13:34-35). They will see something in us they have never seen anywhere else.

Jesus told us that we are to believe him, that we are to walk by faith, we are to believe in what he has accomplished, that he is who he says he is, that he will do what he said he would do (John 6:29, John 8:24). We are to believe this and begin to live as the redeemed people, not as slaves and captives to sin, the world, and the flesh (John 8:34-36); we are to live as people who have been given his righteousness, his Spirit, his indwelling life, his power, and his authority (John 14:11-14). When we really begin to walk by faith, to fight the fight of faith and not yield our faith to the attacks of the world, the flesh, or the enemy, we will realize that this a key that begins to open up the supernatural things of God.

Gifts and Promises. Look at the gifts and promises Jesus gave us. Because of the blood that Jesus shed, God's throne has been opened to us; we may enter and go boldly before the throne of grace, assured of his glad welcome (Hebrews 4:15-16). He is our intercessor, sitting before the Father (Matthew 16:64, Mark 14:62, Hebrews 7:25), so that we can come and make our petitions known (Philippians 4:6). We have direct communion with the Father; there is no veil separating us or a man standing between us (Matthew 27:51, Mark 15:38, Luke 23:45). We may come boldly before the very presence of God and draw his presence.

He not only forgave us, he adopted us and made us his own (Romans 8:15). We have been made sons and daughters of the Most High God (John 1:12-13). We have been made joint heirs with the Son of God; everything that belongs to Jesus now belongs to us (Romans 8:17, Galatians 4:7). We may use Jesus' name, knowing that anything we ask according to his name, the Lord will hear and answer (John 14:14, 15:16, 16:23). God has lavished such a great love on us (1 John 3:1). He has taken the responsibility to be our Father; we are not orphans any longer (John 14:18). We are not alone; he will never leave or forsake us (Hebrews 13:5). He will walk with us and remain with us. Jesus' very life and presence dwells within us (Galatians 4:6).

The same power that raised Jesus from the dead dwells within us (Romans 8:11). He is our Counselor, Helper, Guide, and Teacher (John 14:12,16-17,26). He takes the things of God and makes them known to us. He is the one who guides us. Jesus said, "It is the Father, living in me, who is doing his work" (John 14:10) and that we can do even greater things than him because his Spirit would come and dwell within us (John 14:12). He said it is power from on high; it is the gift of God so that we may be able to operate in the power and wisdom that comes from God (Luke 24:49) rather than in human power and human wisdom. Jesus came to destroy the powers of darkness (Hebrews 2:14, 1 John 3:8). God has given us everything accomplished at the cross and through Jesus' death and resurrection; therefore, the gates of hell cannot prevail against us because he has already defeated them (Matthew 16:18), and we do not need to be intimidated or subject to the forces and powers of darkness because the One who is in us is greater than the one who is in the world (1 John 4:4).

Position and Authority. And that's not all! Jesus has also given us position and authority. We are his ambassadors, his representatives on the earth sent to reconcile the world unto him (2 Corinthians 5:18-20). We are to reveal him, to bear witness to the reality of who he is to this world (Luke 21:12-13, 24:48). We are to be the light in the world that extinguishes the darkness and begins to reveal to people that there is a hope, a life, and a reality they can find (Matthew 5:14). We have been given divine weapons and power to accomplish the work he has given us (2 Corinthians 10:4). He has said that we will be able to trample on snakes and scorpions (Luke 10:19), and that no weapon formed against us shall prosper (Isaiah 54:17). He told us that we are to go into the nations and discipline them in the ways of God, and that we are to see his kingdom established on this earth as it is in Heaven (Matthew 28:19-20). He said that he has given us all the authority that he has in Heaven and on earth so that we may reveal his glory, his righteousness, and his love, and so that we may walk in his power (Matthew 28:18; Luke 10:19).

We are his army. We are sent to destroy the works of the enemy and draw the people of God out of darkness and into the light (1 Peter 2:9). We are called to push back darkness and to see the kingdom of God established and the will of God be done. We are his workmanship, created in Christ Jesus to do good works (Ephesians 2:10). He has called us and gifted us (1 Corinthians 12:28). He has placed his supernatural gifts and calling upon us so that we may see his purposes fulfilled on the earth (2 Thessalonians 1:11), not the purposes of the devil and of darkness. He has given us weapons that have the power to pull down everything that comes against the knowledge of God (2 Corinthians 10:4-5).

We are called to prepare the nations for the Day of the Lord (Matthew 28:19). We are to be ready, watching, and waiting. We are to be his pure and spotless Bride (Matthew 25:1-13, Ephesians 5:27), blowing the trumpet and living in such a way that it attracts people to the reality of who Christ is (Joel 2), and awakening the church so it begins to rise up into the fullness of its stature, its salvation, and the life that Christ gave so that the world may see that Jesus is real and that he is coming soon. He has given us the fullness of his authority, the fullness of his name, the fullness of his Spirit, the fullness of his access to the Father, the fullness of his life, and the fullness of his salvation so that we may go forth and see the will and purposes of God being done across the earth (Colossians 2:9-10).

Is the Church Fulfilling Its Mission?

Is the Church fulfilling its mission? Is it walking in the authority and promises that it has? Is it impacting the nations of the world? With everything God has given us – all his authority, all his gifts, all his promises – are the nations seeing that Jesus Christ is the only hope for what we are facing in this generation and time?

> The Church is in a state of slumber and is not fulfilling its God-given mission.

By looking at the state of the nations, the flood of darkness that is overtaking the nations, and the way the nations are turning away from the ways and wisdom of God, then the answer is without doubt, "No." There are many things we can list and blame as the cause of this, but one thing that has become clear is that the Church is in a state of slumber and is not fulfilling its God-given mission.

The Church Is in Slumber

God has given the Church more than 2,000 years to go to the nations and fulfill its mandate. But the Day is near and the judgments are beginning to come upon the earth. Wickedness is suffocating the nations. People no longer know the difference between right and wrong, holy and unholy, because the line has become so blurred. There is a rise of deception and the time is growing late.

But God continues to uphold his plan of redemption: he is issuing a wake-up call to the Church that is being heard all around the world. A remnant is rising up that is willing to surrender their lives to God. They are willing to allow him to set them apart and to use them to continue to awaken the Bride and prepare God's people to complete the mission he has given the Church.

There is hope, however. God is coming back for a victorious Church, a pure and spotless Bride. God is continuing to uphold his plan of redemption.

The Wake-Up Call
Jesus told the disciples a parable about the end times:

> *"At that time the kingdom of heaven will be like ten virgins who took their lamps and went out to meet the bridegroom. Five of them were foolish and five were wise. The foolish ones took their lamps but did not take any oil with them. The wise, however, took oil in jars along with their lamps. The bridegroom was a long time in coming, and they all became drowsy and fell asleep. At midnight the cry rang out: 'Here's the bridegroom! Come out to meet him!' Then all the virgins woke up and trimmed their lamps. The foolish ones said to the wise, 'Give us some of your oil; our lamps are going out.' 'No,' they replied, 'there may not be enough for both us and you. Instead, go to those who sell oil and buy some for yourselves.' But while they were on their way to buy the oil, the bridegroom arrived. The virgins who were ready went in with him to the wedding banquet. And the door was shut. Later the others also came. 'Sir! Sir!' they said. 'Open the door for us!' But he replied, 'I tell you the truth, I don't know you.' Therefore keep watch, because you do not know the day or the hour."*
>
> Matthew 25:1-13

The Lord said that because he is going to tarry in his coming, the Church would fall asleep. The people of God would go into a state of slumber, weariness, loss of sight of his mission, a state where we do not have the same fervor and devotion we had in the past.

But he, being faithful, will come in the night and begin to issue a wake-up call. It is clear that God is issuing that wake-up call RIGHT NOW (this is his timing). We are seeing two evidences of the timing of the Lord. One is that we are seeing God shake the earth. We have mentioned throughout these chapters all the things that are coming at the nations to perplex, confound, and shake – they are coming and coming and coming. It is confounding the nations as they try to determine how to deal with the perplexity of the problems they are facing, whether it is natural disasters, terrorism, economic instability, diseases we have never heard of before, or other things. As all these significant and frequent events are happening, it is as if an alarm is going off across the nations, causing people to say, "We must begin to seek the Lord."

Second, God is seeking to raise our faith so that in the midst of this shaking we will begin to turn and look to the Lord. As we do that, we begin to realize that all across this world, God is moving in transforming power in the nations.

In parts of the world, as people are seeking the Lord with all their hearts, he is moving in such size and power that it is almost like modern-day Bible stories. Coral reefs are coming back to life in a matter of weeks, agriculture is producing greater quantities and size than ever before, dictators and drug lords are being brought down, scourges and diseases like AIDS are being wiped out. The presence of the Lord is being drawn so close in some cities that the sins of the land are being healed; drug addictions, prostitution, and drunkenness are being eradicated. It is like a whole generation is being cleansed and restored to God. The Lord is provoking our faith to believe him to transform whole cities and nations like no other time in history.

God is also speaking to people in every part of the world. He is raising up prayer movements all across nations. People are hungering for transformation in their cities, unity is being sought after in thousands and thousands of cities across the world. There is a cry going out in the Body of Christ in the nations that we need God, and they are beginning to go after God with greater desire and hunger. The trumpet is sounding and God is sending out an alarm into the nations of the world.

As this alarm is going out, we must remain alert and watchful. Jesus did not say that the virgins – the Church – would slumber until the end. When the wake-up call comes, there will be a time of rising up and a time of preparation. We may recognize that we have been in a state of slumber, but let our confidence be that as this wake-up call goes out, God's grace will be with us to take us beyond anywhere we could take ourselves.

God is beginning to tell us that it is time to arise, time to seek him, and time to go after him with all our heart, soul, mind, and strength.

Because of this, we want to begin to ask ourselves, "How do we allow God to position us so we continue to seek after him and allow him to make us ready and not be pulled back into the chaos and slumber that is going on in our day and time?"

GROUP DISCUSSION QUESTIONS

General Discussion Questions (for whole group)
1. What is the general teaching we are seeking to grasp in this chapter?
2. What changes do we/you need to make in response to the lesson this week (in actions, mindset, etc)?
3. What has been the never-changing purpose of God since Creation?
4. What were the intentions of God in raising up the nation of Israel? How were they to impact the nations?
5. How did Israel stray from God? What were the consequences of their disobedience?
6. What is the similarity between Israel and the Church today? Explain.
7. What has God given the Church to fulfill its mission? Make a list as a group. Is the Church operating in the fullness of what we have been give? Explain.
8. How would you define slumber and how do you see it in the Church?
9. Discuss the parable of the ten virgins (Matthew 25:1-13).

Personal Application Questions (for breakout groups)
1. What did the Lord impress upon your heart as you read this week?
2. How is God sending a wake-up call to you?
3. Do you see slumber trying to subdue or dampen that wake-up call?
4. How can we pray for one another to be awakened and prepared as the Day of the Lord draws near?

Weekly Prayer Targets:
1. Pray for a level of understanding and discernment regarding the signs of the times and for fearless hearts that know God.

2. Pray for awakening in the Church so that we would not be caught unaware and slumbering, but ready for Christ's return.
3. Pray that we would understand our covenant position and begin to rise up and walk in the love, wisdom, righteousness, and authority of Jesus Christ.
4. Ask God to instill in you hope without wavering and steadfastness to endure.

Section 2

The Call
of the Hour

Chapter 4

The Key to Winning the Battle

A Word From the Lord to John Mulinde, September 10, 2001:
*"Set yourself apart for me. Allow me to work deeply in your life
to break the hooks the world has in you. I will help you overcome
things you cannot overcome by yourself. I will cause your life to
be separated from everything that hinders you from excelling in
me. I will lift you above the influences of your world and set you
free from its bonds and limitations. I will give you authority over
nations and peoples. I will cause people to be drawn to my light in
your life in a way you could have never imagined possible. I will
cause my Word through you to be much more effective than ever
before. I will equip your life to accomplish things far beyond your
own imagination, things otherwise impossible for you today. All
I am seeking is a vessel set apart for me, totally separated from
the allurements and dictates of the world, and fully yielded to my
will. This was the secret of the early Church. It was the secret of
everyone I ever used in generations gone by. It is still the secret to
my power today. Whoever will yield their lives wholly to me in this
manner, I will always honor.*

John 12:24-26

The evening of September 10, 2001, will remain forever stamped on
my memory. That night, while I was praying, the Lord spoke words to
me that were destined to radically change my life and ministry.

I was in Seattle, WA (USA), at the invitation of my friend George Otis,
Jr, the producer of the well-known *Transformations* videos. These
videos document communities all over the world that are being
transformed by the power of God. Thousands of these videos have
been distributed worldwide.[1]

---

[1]To purchase these and other videos produced by George Otis, Jr, visit
www.glowtorch.org.

There are testimonies from all over the world about how the *Transformation* videos have created spiritual hunger in people from all walks of life, inspiring them to seek God more, both individually and corporately. These videos have helped Christians worldwide to come to appreciate the power of prayer and of working in unity. A determination to bring about community transformation is sweeping through churches everywhere.

I had travelled to Seattle to make a recording that, along with others, was going to be used in a follow-up to the *Transformations II* video. George Otis had invited several leaders from across the world who had been part of the process of community transformation. George had brought us together to share the lessons and core values we had learned.

George's desire was to identify a body of core values that are evident in each case of transformation and that could be of help to those in other communities in the nations who are hungry for transformation. It was hoped that as intercessors studied and pursued these core values, God would honor their faith and guide them into strategies that would transform their own communities. This is a cause that I fully believe in. I am sure it is God-inspired, and I would give everything and anything to see it succeed.

I had arrived in Seattle on September 8, 2001, and began to prepare myself for the recording, which was to begin on September 11. On the evening of September 10, I was praying and interceding for the following day's program. As I prayed, a heavy burden came on my heart. It suddenly occurred to me that we were actually taking an immense responsibility on ourselves. I became aware that there are millions of God's people who have watched the *Transformations* videos. Many more will watch them in the future, and their cry will be, "Lord, for the sake of our cities and nations, just show us how to do it and we will go for it, whatever the cost!" These are people who will be willing do anything to see similar results in their own communities. All they need is some clear guidance as to how to go about it, and the recordings we were about to make would hopefully provide that.

On the one hand, my heart felt extremely excited about this opportunity. Without a doubt the core values, shared from various transformed communities by people with first-hand experience, would be a great and invaluable treasure. On the other hand, however, I realized that if the right state of heart is not attained by the seekers – if they do not see their own part in the sickness of their lands and cry out for healing to start with them – they would never have access to the power to change their lands for God.

They could be presented with all the principles of transformation, and maybe even implement them zealously, yet still see no results. This is because people seeking a quick solution very often miss the most obvious thing: they ignore the basic works of brokenness, total surrender to God, and rejection of the status quo.

I am convinced that communities are transformed when a few people in them reach a point of yearning for God so desperately that they will pay any price to see his intervention in the land. This is the same holy desperation that has driven all past revivalists in church history the world over. However, experience shows that, rather than allow God to deal with their own hearts first, which would equip them to impact their worlds with their lives, most people today opt for the strategies, methods, or formulas that they believe will produce certain spiritual experiences.

> Communities are transformed when a few people in them reach a point of yearning for God so desperately that they will pay any price to see his intervention in the land.

Therefore, as I pondered this reality during my prayer time, the burden on my heart was: How do we move God's people beyond concentrating on methods alone, to focus instead on experiencing real personal transformation from the inside out, which would progress from the individual to the community? I felt convinced that this was the cry of God's heart: to bring people to such a dynamic encounter with him that he could work powerfully through them to change their nations.

Even as I continued to pray, I had within me a deep fear: What if, even after people have embraced the values we share, they still did not see breakthrough in their communities because they have ignored the work necessary within their own hearts? What about those who have tried every strategy and pattern they have heard about and have now become weary? They would not be keen on trying anything new or stretching their faith any further! They need to know why, after all these years of effort, they now find themselves facing an impasse.

Knowing the skeptics of this present world, and the speed with which theologians and scholars rush to discredit everyone and everything at the slightest provocation, I felt really jealous for the noble cause we had come to Seattle to work for. I did not want this work to be ridiculed in any way or to come to naught. I desired with all my heart to see it accomplish its intended purpose. I did not know what to do or how we could avoid what I was fearing, to I cried out the more to God, "Lord, you know our hearts. You know that all we desire is to see you glorified throughout the earth. Please guide this whole process to produce what will make your heart rejoice in your people in the nations."

I felt strongly in my heart that what God had begun to do through George Otis, Jr, was intended to inspire such faith in God's people worldwide that they would break age-old strongholds over their nations and cities, and this would open the door for God-glorifying revivals throughout the world. I felt an undeniable conviction that not only is this dream possible, but that this is actually the ordained hour for it to happen.

As I continued in my prayer and travail, I reflected on the nations to which I had travelled in Africa, Europe, the Americas, the Middle East, the Far East, and other parts of the world. There is no denying that some real awakening is going on in all of these regions. There is undeniably an increased volume of prayer, and more and more people are becoming hungry for God. People are becoming increasingly aware that God requires them to step into deeper waters.

The reason I felt so desperate was not because I was not seeing any results in my own ministry in these nations; on the contrary, a lot has happened beyond even my own expectations. However, I could also see in my spirit that there are strongholds deeply and manifestly entrenched in the lifestyles of people in every region of the world. These are so deeply rooted that it appears almost impossible to bring communities to the point where they can experience God's glorious power of revival. There are so many things that stand in the way of genuine nation-sweeping revivals, such as culture, tradition, mindsets, indulgent lifestyles, and the general worldview of people today. I was deeply aware of how the nations and their peoples – including even the Christian believers – are held in captivity to their social systems. These bondages have become so much a part of us that we scarcely notice how they cause our lives to stray from what is in the Word of God. Instead, we conform to the world around us.

When I compared the extent of the revival that I sensed in my spirit God was ready to pour out over the nations, and what was practically happening on the ground all over the world, I was left with no doubt at all that there is need for a major break from our present lifestyles if we are going to see God's glory cover the nations.

I suddenly felt heavily weighed down by the realization that in every region, whether it be in Europe or Africa, America or Asia, or even in communities where a degree of transformation has already occurred, such as in Guatemala or Uganda, the world system has such a strong hold on God's people that the Church has come to adjust its expectations to only what seems possible within the system.

As the Word is being ministered, preachers labor so hard to fit within the system that what ends up being released is often so watered down that it loses the impact needed to change our world. Doctrines have been created to explain it all away and make God's people feel comfortable in this mediocrity. A subtle veil is separating today's Church from the fullness of its divine inheritance here on earth.

As a result, this latter Church of God is only a shadow of the former Church seen in the first century. Many have even come to accept and believe that this is all that can be expected from God today. However, I believe that no one who has ever gazed on the face of the Lord would settle for such a conclusion! We know that his heart is craving to do much more for the human race than anything we have witnessed so far. It has been prophesied that an end-time worldwide revival will occur in all nations that will surpass the glory of the first works, and for sure this must happen. It does not matter how impossible it may appear, it has to happen!

As these thoughts raced through my mind on that night in Seattle, it suddenly struck my heart that there was something God was trying to open my eyes to see. If the prophecy of God's end-time revival is to come true and if the knowledge of God's glory is to cover the earth as the waters cover the sea (Habakkuk 2:14 & Isaiah 11:9), then there must be a way around all the obstacles we see in the nations.

I began to search for the key that would unlock the door of nations and cities to allow God to invade today's world with his glorious transforming power. My mind raced back through the Bible to seek for answers. I was strongly impressed by stories of God breaking seemingly impossible world systems to transform nations and communities in such a way that whole empires bowed down in acknowledgement of his name.

Biblical Examples of Transformed Nations

There are many, many Biblical examples of transformed nations.

- When Moses confronted Pharaoh to secure the Hebrews' release from Egypt, a whole nation was redeemed from a seemingly impenetrable system (1 Kings 8:51).
- Through Samuel, in a time of great spiritual barrenness, the nation of Israel experienced revival and transformation. A land in which the Word of God was scarce and in which there was no one with a vision was suddenly filled with the Word of God and all the nations knew about it (1 Samuel 3:1).
- Because of the faith Daniel, Meshach, Shadrach, and Abednego the supreme rulers in Babylon declared openly, on several different occasions, that there was no God like the God of Israel, and that all people in the empire should honor him (Daniel 3:16-18).
- God even intervened in the life of Nebuchadnezzar to the point of breaking his pride and causing him to acknowledge his name (Daniel 4:34). This is still the same God we serve!
- The same thing happened in the days of King Josiah, and of the prophets Elijah, Jeremiah, and John the Baptist (2 Kings 22:19-20, 1 Kings 19, Jeremiah 3:12-13, Matthew 3:11).

As these stories streamed through my mind, my heart began to race. Yes! I knew without a doubt that the Spirit of God was leading me to discover a gem I had never touched before, something that might unlock the door to the transformation of nations worldwide. Faced with our world system today there seems to be no hope of turning whole nations to God. But is that not how it must also have appeared in the days of Moses, Daniel, Samuel, and Elijah?

Consider the challenges facing the Apostles as they started out to fulfill the Great Commission. They lived in a system deeply entrenched in religious beliefs that had been developed through God dealings with them for several millennia:

- They had the law, received supernaturally by Moses on the mountain.
- They had the prophets, who under the Holy Spirit had dealt so powerfully with their forefathers.
- They had a history rich with examples of God's miracles, both in their own land and in foreign lands.

These were the foundation blocks of their beliefs, formed out of thousands of years of documented evidence that God was undeniably and vividly involved in it all.

But it was to these very people that the Apostles had to take the gospel message, proclaiming that there was no true salvation in all the age-old beliefs they trusted in, that no one would ever see God unless they put their faith in a little-known, rather unconventional, self-proclaimed prophet names Jesus. The Apostles had to convince the Jews that this same Jesus, who had lived among them only a short while ago, was truly the long-awaited Messiah of the Jews. That they were no longer to follow the law but to follow him, the Messiah, and to receive the Spirit of God by faith in him. That he was the King of the Jews who came in the line of David, the Judge of all the world, and the embodiment of everything the prophets had ever prophesied!

In addition, they also had to convince the Jews that this Jesus was actually the Son of God, literally equal to God himself, that he existed in the beginning before the creation of anything, that he was with God and is actually God himself, and that he is the author of all things and without him nothing was made that has been made. They had to prove all of this to the Jews, who had known their God for thousands of years under different terms. Wow! That is a challenging task!

Surely, the idea that eternal life could only be found in the Nazarene, who had just been killed openly and publicly as a criminal in Jerusalem, was no more appealing to the people of that day than our claims about Jesus are to our world today. But the Apostles went forth in the power of the Lord and successfully proclaimed the Good News to their generation. Who can deny that they made a life-changing impact everywhere they went?

Consider Paul and the other evangelists who went throughout the pagan nations preaching the gospel of Jesus Christ to people who had traditionally worshipped everything but the God of Israel since time immemorial. Remember that as a nation, Israel was under Roman rule, both militarily and politically. Culturally and intellectually they were under the shadow of the Greeks. Religiously they were often ridiculed because, unlike other nations who were rich in many gods (and who had a god for every need), the Israelites had only one God to whom they turned for everything – and at that time it did not even appear that he was doing very much for them; they were under foreign domination.

In all senses the Israelites were underdogs who stood to be pitied by those who considered themselves much more "civilized" peoples (see, for example, Acts 17:16-25, 30-32). And yet it was to these same people that Jesus gave the mandate of the Great Commission: "Go therefore and make disciples of all the nations" (Matthew 28:19).

Never before in all history had anyone attempted to bring the peoples of the nations, with all their diversity of cultures and beliefs, to believe in one God. But this is what Jesus was demanding of his followers: "Go therefore and make disciples of all nations...teaching them to observe all things that I have commanded you" (Matthew 28:19). Some of these nations were richer, stronger, more civilized, and more enlightened than Israel was perceived to be. Others were purely barbaric, deeply entrenched in satanic worship, idolatry, and even human sacrifice, which their forefathers had practiced over many generations.

The apostles were commissioned to go to these nations and convince them that they needed to change their beliefs, break out of their traditional world systems and lifestyles, and put their faith in the one Lord called Jesus Christ, King of the Jews. And if they would do that, all their sins would be forgiven and they would inherit eternal life! This same Jesus who had died and rose from the dead would come back and take them to heaven to live with him in glory forever and ever. How about that for a challenge?

> One of the most amazing things about the early Church is the degree of success they experienced in turning nations upside down for Jesus.

Compare their task with ours today. Without a doubt, theirs was as impossible a task as any we have ever faced, and yet one of the most amazing things about the early Church is the degree of success they experienced in turning nations upside down for Jesus. Despite all the odds against them, the early Church took the gospel with power. They broke through barriers and systems, and brought people to Jesus with incredible results. Nations of totally heathen people were radically changed as they were exposed to the Gospel. Traditions were dismantled, customs were abandoned, and religions were discarded. In some cases, even whole economic systems collapsed as people turned away from idolatry and the trades that depended on it (see, for example, Acts 19:18-19, 23-34). The Apostles made such an impact on their world that the unbelievers of their day testified about them, "These who have turned the world upside down have come here, too" (Acts 17:6).

We should believe that if they did it then, we can do it, too. Yes! We can transform our nation for Christ today just as they did 2,000 years ago. After all, we serve the same Lord and he has given us the same Great Commission.

Why Are We Not Seeing This Happening?

Doesn't the Church of today have the same anointing as the early Church? Don't we have the same power as the Acts Church to see cities turned upside down and revival come to the nations? Yes! The same Holy Spirit who dwelt in them is the very same Spirit who dwells in us today.

As I pondered these things that night in Seattle, I cried out even more that God would show me the key our forerunners had that we are missing today. I was on my face before the Lord a good part of that night, pouring out my heart in anguish.

"Lord," I cried out to him, "what is it that has weakened the Church of our day so much? We don't even seem to be bothered by the growing moral decay of our day! What must we do to break the power of wickedness that is holding the nations in such a vicious grip? Is there no way to bring spiritual liberation to the people of our day? Lord, are you not the same God who worked with the early Church to break the same powers over whole nations? Could you have done that yesterday and yet not be willing to do the same today? But, Lord, you are no respecter of persons, and the Great Commission you gave to them is the very same commission you have given us. The same promise you spoke to them in Matthew 28:20 still applies in our day: 'And lo, I am with you always, even to the end of the age.'"

"Lord, you prayed for us as much as for them, 'As you sent me into the world, I also have sent them into the world...I do not pray for these alone, but also for those who will believe in me through their word' (John 17:17, 20). Moreover, you promised in your Word that, 'The glory of this latter house shall be greater than of the former" (Haggai 2:9, NKJV). And again you said, 'For the earth will be filled with the knowledge of the glory of the LORD, as the waters cover the sea' (Habakkuk 2:14). Father, are we wrong to believe you for greater works in our day than those you accomplished in the first century? Surely what we are seeing today is a far cry from what they witnessed in the first century. Lord, please give me the revelation I am crying out for. What was the early Church's secret, and how can we rediscover it?"

This was the essence of my heart cry as I pleaded before the Lord. The pressure of knowing that the next day I was going to do a recording sharing lessons learned in community transformation weighed heavily on my heart. I had been asked to talk about the role of prayer in community transformation. I knew that the values I had learned are gems in kingdom building. I knew also that what the other speakers had already shared from their own experience was invaluable. Nevertheless, there was no doubt in my heart that I was being invited by the Holy Spirit to explore an area whose significance reached far beyond what I would need for the following morning's recording. I felt a burning conviction deep in my heart that if I followed the leading I was sensing, I was about to embark on something that would change my entire approach to ministry and maybe even my whole life. I did not have the slightest idea about what was coming my way.

The Lord Answers

As I pondered these thoughts, the Spirit of the Lord began to pour his word into my heart. It came as a burning fire blazing through my heart, strong and clear. I have tried as best as I can to put it into words:

> "Understand that the world and its systems have been changing and will continue to change. New developments are affecting the way nations are acting concerning their destinies and the way their peoples are responding to God. But besides all that, you need to understand at this very moment that there is going to be a major shift in the heavenly realm. The powers in the heavenly realm over the entire world are going to shift irreversibly. This is going to cause fundamental changes in world affairs, which will also affect your labors in the Gospel. These changes will affect every area of life. They will affect the political atmosphere of the entire world, the economic and social atmosphere, and every level of human relations and of survival.

> The system of the world as you know it is falling apart. The time is coming when every foundation that people are used to will give way to something new. The coming system will tighten its grip on the peoples of all nations. People will increasingly be driven by the

events around them, and these will drive them further and further away from the place of grace. If you are going to see a major breakthrough in the nations, then you need to understand the connection between the world system in the land and the way the people of that land respond to the Gospel. You also need to understand how important it is for you to disentangle yourself from the grip of the world around you. You are in the world but not of the world."

At the time I did not realize how much this word related to the 9/11 disaster and the changes that would follow it. I also did not realize what a major shift in the heavenly realm the events of the day would create.

It slowly dawned on me that people are products of their society and will live according to its dictates and expectations. They will be constrained and limited by the world system in that society, which also means that as the world system changes within that society, the people living within it will also change their attitude toward life. This also goes for their attitude toward God and the Gospel. Consequently, even when those people have a hunger for God, they will be continually hindered and limited in their quest and experience of God according to the dictates of their society, unless these can be broken and the people set free.

> Even when people have a hunger for God, they will be continually hindered and limited in their quest and experience of God unless they can be set free from the dictates of their society.

These kinds of changes have already begun in many nations of the world. This is already evident in Europe, where the world system and worldview have changed immensely since the two world wars, from being a fundamentally Christian land to the present so-called "post-Christian Europe." Consider how this has affected the corporate attitude of Europe's people toward God and the Gospel in these nations. This not only affects nonbelievers, it also affects the believers in the depth of their faith and their experience of God.

It is especially sad when you consider the younger generations, who are being born into a society whose values have drifted so far away from God. The boundary between right and wrong has all but been removed. Values are totally confused, so good is called evil and evil good. Consider how this affects the openness of these younger people to the Gospel. They are victims of history!

That night, the Lord showed me prophetically that there will come a time (very soon) when the Church, as it is today, will not be able to have any kind of impact on people living in today's world system, no matter what it tries. The very people it is trying to reach will consider its message irrelevant.

Even some who are part of the Church as it is today will turn away and abandon it, believing that it provides no answers to the pressing issues of their lives. The methods used by the Church today (the systems, strategies, and approach of ministry) within the present world system will totally lose their impact. These methods will no longer be applicable or relevant. The world will simply ignore the Church, regarding it as an irrelevant institution.

This day is not far away. If we are going to make any impact at such a time as this, we need to totally change our attitude and approach.

So What Should We Do?

I cried out in my heart to the Lord, "Oh God, what must we do? How can we prepare for what is coming and overcome it?" The response was quick and direct:

> *"Set yourself apart for me. Allow me to work deeply in your life to break the hooks the world has in you. I will help you overcome things you cannot overcome by yourself. I will cause your life to be separated from everything that hinders you from excelling in me. I will lift you above the influences of your world and set you free from its bonds and limitations. I will give you authority over nations and peoples. I will cause people to be drawn to my light in your life in a way you could have never imagined possible. I will cause my Word through you to be much more effective than ever before. I will equip your life to accomplish things far beyond your own imagination, things otherwise impossible for you today. All I am seeking is a vessel set apart for me, totally separated from the allurements and dictates of the world, and fully yielded to my will.*

If you want to know, this was the secret of the early Church. It was the secret of everyone I ever used in generations gone by. It is still the secret to my power today. Whoever will yield their lives wholly to me in this manner, I will always honor" (John 12:24-26).

Set Yourself Apart for Me

Most people who genuinely want to pursue the Lord in the set apart journey will tend to respond to his call in the way they understand. Even the most pious men like Samuel did this. God asked him to anoint the next king of Israel from Jesse's home. He assumed according to his human understanding that he would be anointing the oldest son. Similarly, when I heard those words, "Set yourself apart for me," I felt a pang go through my heart, yet I did not grasp their full meaning immediately. Because I had a preconceived idea of what this level of consecration required, I thought that the Lord was calling me into a time of fasting and prayer.

This is God's call to you:

"Set yourself apart for me and allow me to prepare you for the times that are coming. Only those set apart for me will be able to overcome in the times ahead."

I thought He was asking me to lay down my plans for a while and separate myself to seek his face in seclusion for a period of time, so I cried out immediately, "Lord, I will do it. I will start whenever you tell me. How many days should I fast? Lord, I am willing to fast as long as you want me to. I am willing to go any distance to gain this breakthrough."

But I received no answer. There was just an unnaturally pregnant silence in the Spirit that left me with no doubt that I had misconceived something.

Although I prayed some more, the Spirit of the Lord did not say anything else that night. Before dawn, I again resumed my prayer to the Lord: "Father, give us the nations. Show us what will break the prison gates to set your people free." Again the word of the Lord came to me, throwing more light on the earlier words:

> *"The world is changing faster than you are adjusting, and the issues you are dealing with are getting more and more challenging. As a result you are getting caught up in the sway of the world. So many of my servants have already gone down this path and their work is increasingly losing impact. I have spoken to them, calling*

them apart to me, but they are so busy with the things the world has thrust before them that they keep putting me off. They hear my call in their hearts but they are so engrossed with what they are doing that they have no time to heed my call. Some of what they are doing is my work, but it is losing power because it is no longer coping with the trends in the world. Some of them are so busy trying to serve my people that they do not realize they are drifting further and further away from me. My heart is grieving because I am losing them to the power and pulls of the world. Unless you set yourself apart for me and allow me to work deeply within you, you will also drift along in the same way. You will not even be able to stand in the days ahead.

The enemy is raising his stakes. There are things that appeared harmless to you in the past that are now going to act like fierce hooks holding you back and not letting go. You will struggle hard to do what you know is right, but the hindrances in your life will be so strong that you will fall short of the mark.

Pay heed and hear my call. Set yourself apart for me! This is my call to you. It is my call to all my people. Go out and say it out loud to all my people, whether they hear or not. Go and be a witness to them. Tell them that this is my call of the hour! Set yourselves apart for me and allow me to prepare you for the times that are coming. Only those set apart for me will be able to overcome in the times ahead."

GROUP DISCUSSION QUESTIONS

General Discussion Questions (for whole group)

1. What is the general teaching we are seeking to grasp in this chapter?
2. What changes do we/you need to make in response to the lesson this week (in actions, mindset, etc)?
3. What is your understanding of the world system around you? How would you define it?
4. What is your understanding of being set apart?
5. Why is being set apart a key to personal revival and transformation? What is the secret to transformation in our cities and nations?

Personal Application Questions (for breakout groups)

1. What did the Lord impress upon your heart as you read this week?
2. How do you see the world system pressuring and entangling you?
3. Have you heard the call from God to be set apart? What are the things that are keeping you from responding? How are you putting God off?
4. How can we pray for one another to get past this?

Weekly Prayer Targets:

1. Ask God to show you your part in the sickness of your land. Cry out to God for the healing to start with you.
2. Ask the Lord to begin to reveal to you attitudes, traditions, or cultural values that you may have become so steeped in that you don't realize how they are an idol or a compromise to his standards.

Chapter 5

The Call of the Hour

A Word From the Lord to John Mulinde, September 11, 2001:
"This call of separation unto me is not just to you alone. This is the call of the hour for my people worldwide. Surrender and set yourselves apart unto me. I will separate you from your weaknesses. I will make you the people I will use to overturn nations and cities in these last days. I will gather in your loved ones, transform your communities, and bring glory to my name. I want you to tell this to my people everywhere you go."

When the time came for me to leave for my recording on the morning of September 11, 2001, I went down to the hotel lobby to meet the lady who had come to pick me up. The first words she said to me were, "John, isn't it terrible what has happened?" Perplexed, I asked what she meant. Surprised that I was not aware of what had happened in New York City that morning, she told me that a passenger plane had crashed into one of the Twin Towers of the World Trade Center! At the time she was not aware of the full extent of the devastation. She led me to the television in the hotel lobby so I could see the bizarre spectacle for myself. My first thoughts were, "God Almighty, how many of the people in that tower were spiritually ready to meet their death?"

We then drove to the venue where I was to do the recording. When we got there, we learned that not just one, but both towers of the World Trade Center had been hit. Each tower had been hit by a separate plane. It became clear to all of us that this was no accident. It was a terrorist attack. We also soon learned that another plane had hit the Pentagon and yet another had crashed in a field in Pennsylvania. There was confusion everywhere. The atmosphere was tense. George Otis, Jr, sent a message that in the circumstances he could not come to do his recording. It was suggested that I go ahead with mine, which I did, but I don't think I made much sense. My mind was on other things.

As soon as I could, I returned to my hotel room and began to follow the news on TV. Seeing those pictures and the shock of the nation of America, I could not help but be swallowed up by grief. I have seen suffering before in Uganda, not for just one day, but for years. Even though I had grown up under much suffering, never before had I witnessed such heartbreak and emptiness as I experienced that week in the United States. One could feel the angry shock of a nation whose sense of security had been irreversibly shaken. The sense of being a safe haven had been violated, leaving fear and panic in the air.

I felt personally affected. The pain in my heart was acute and grew more and more intense as I watched the details unfold. In fact, I was so traumatized by the whole thing that for 3 weeks after I left the United States I could not sleep through the night. I would fall asleep for 1 or 2 hours and then remain awake for the rest of the night. The pictures of the terrorist attacks would stream through my mind, as well as thoughts of the bereaved who were mourning their loved ones in shock and agony.

On the night of the attack on the World Trade Center, as I watched TV, thoughts began to take shape in my mind that brought some under-standing of the Lord's call for me to be set apart unto Him. Watching the repeated images from "Ground Zero" in New York City, my at-tention was riveted by the New York Fire Department rescue work-ers. These men, who were frantically digging into the mountains of rubble in the hope of finding survivors, were the picture of bravery itself. They were working under very dangerous conditions. Many of their colleagues had already lost their lives in the effort, and they too were at risk of being buried alive by the rubble at any moment.

I marveled at the courage and determination of these firefighters. The TV showed one who had worked straight through for many long hours without a break. When asked if he did not think he needed to take a rest, he replied, "Someone in there may be hanging on, de-pending on us to get to them in the next few minutes. How can I rest knowing the possibility of that?"

I heard of another man, also a rescue worker, who had run up into one of the towers to help people escape before it collapsed. Someone shouted to him to abandon the rescue effort and get out because it was too dangerous. The rescue worker replied that he couldn't leave as long as there were people in there whose lives he could save. It was reported that he called his wife on the phone, telling her that he didn't know whether he was going to make it out of the building. He wanted her to know that he had always loved her and enjoyed being married to her. He never came out alive!

Hundreds of other rescue workers perished as they tried to save lives. Many of them died courageously and sacrificially, knowingly risking their own safety for the sake of others. I marveled at the commitment, courage, determination, and selflessness of these men. They could have spared their own lives if they had chosen to, but they did not. As I watched, the Spirit of the Lord said to me,

> *"What those men are doing today is not a result of a decision that they made this morning. It is not a decision they made as a reaction to the tragedy you are watching now. Many years ago, each of them made a decision to join a profession that would demand selfless service to save others' lives."*

That decision shaped their destiny. They underwent training and preparation for crises of all sorts. They allowed themselves to be trained (some may call it "programmed") to cope with extreme conditions of tension and danger. In their training, any personal weaknesses that would easily compromise them were identified and dealt with. The discipline that would make them strong enough and bold enough to deal with any circumstance they might face was steadily incorporated into their inner fabric.

None of this was achieved in a matter of days. It took time to slowly change their priorities and values. They learned to despise the things that matter so much to other people, the things that would hold them back. They learned to uphold values that most people dismiss as too high. In other words, *a long time ago they had set themselves apart for such a task and time as this.* When the day came, they were there and they were ready!

If placed in similar circumstances, many well-meaning people would just turn and run for their lives without feeling any sense of guilt, and that is precisely what happened in New York. It was the most sensible thing for any sane person to do, to run for their life! Yet the attitude of these firefighters was different. To them the logical thing was not to run away, but to plunge themselves into the danger and save a life while the opportunity existed. The only reason they were able to do this was because long ago they invested time and effort in preparing their lives to function in and above circumstances such as these. They were surrendered, set apart to their profession – their calling – in order to overcome their world. When the impossible situation came, they effectively saved many, many lives. Today, these once unknown men are celebrated as heroes.

As I pondered what the Spirit of the Lord was saying to me, he very softly said,

> *"The call to be set apart is not about going away for a few days of fasting and prayer. It is a call to a long-term sowing into a new lifestyle. It is a call out of one lifestyle, which looks so logical and right to other people, into another lifestyle programmed for victory and the ability to stand when others would fall or turn and run. What the nations need today is a new breed of God's people that live their lives above the constraints that hold others back. People who have learned to despise the things that trap and hold back everyone else. People who have allowed themselves to have a dynamic encounter with God through which the Lord himself makes them vessels of honor.*
>
> *If you will allow yourself to start on this journey, I will work deeply in your life to do to you what you cannot do for yourself. I will change your attitude toward life. I will separate you from things that weaken your heart. And I will make you able to stand where many would just fall or give in to pressure. You will be an overcomer; then I will position you to help my people worldwide in the times ahead."*

It was not an audible voice, but it was very powerful. Sometimes God speaks in ways that even words cannot describe.

Being Set Apart

There was now a new piece to the puzzle. If being set apart is not about a few days of fasting, then what indeed was it about and how did one do it? Another illustration soon came my way. As I continued to watch the news updates, I was deeply disturbed by the repeated pictures of the terrorist planes being flown straight into the Twin Towers of the World Trade Center.

I asked myself, "What were those pilots thinking during those last moments? They were aware that all the passengers on board, as

The call to be set apart is not about going away for a few days of fasting and prayer; it is a call to a long-term sowing into a new lifestyle.

well as the people inside the World Trade Center, were innocent unsuspecting individuals with loved ones waiting to see them back home. What went through the minds of the pilots in those final moments as they approached the towers, watching those towers draw closer and closer, and knowing that they themselves were going to die along with everyone else? How could anybody be so heartless? How did their hearts become so hardened that they did not flinch in the slightest from what they were about to do?"

Then my thoughts changed direction. These men were dedicated. They had invested a great deal of time and money in their education and flight training. They could have made good money and lived a good life that most people would envy. What on earth would cause such individuals to give all this up and choose to fly a jet plane into high-rise buildings to sure, inescapable death?

Suddenly my mind cleared, and the answers seemed to unfold. Those men were not acting on impulse. They did not wake up that morning and decide that it might be a good idea to undertake a suicide mission. It was not something impulsive they did because they saw an opportunity. Like the New York City firefighters, these men must have made a choice many years before. Each of them had a moment in their life when they decided to lay down their lives for a cause they believed in. It doesn't matter that you and I don't believe in their cause. What is important here is to note the principle that paved the way for such a mission.

When these men joined the ranks of their fanatical organizations, they knew what they were signing up for. They went and trained. They learned to overcome fear, emotions, and anything else that would hamper their suicidal mission. They distanced themselves from the things that mean everything to the rest of us, the things that are important to us as "normal people." They learned to despise and deny the values that would cause any of the rest of us to pause and reconsider. Their priorities in life were grossly altered, and they lived a life that was already given over to death. Their cause was all that mattered to them.

Some of them even had families, but they kept their mission secret from their wives and children. They gave up a life that other men labor for. When the moment came for their hideous mission, they did not pull back. They had no thoughts of retreat even as they approached their sure death. They destroyed thousands of lives without flinching.

Like the New York City rescue workers, what made all this possible was the initial long-term investment they had made in becoming the people they were. There was a moment in their lives when they separated themselves from the influences of their worlds and laid down their lives for a cause they were willing to live and die for. They overcame all human weaknesses that would have held them back through the discipline of a life sown into a cause.

They were focused on their goals. They went through life involving themselves in all normal activity; they did not allow anything to distract them from their life purpose. When the time came to answer the call to do what seems to us impossible, they shook off everything else and let nothing hold them back. Neither their financial achievement, educational achievement, or their families, wives, children, or girlfriends held them back from what they considered the purpose of their life. They were set apart to overcome their world.

It All Makes Sense

It all began to make sense to me. I began to understand the call of God to be set apart unto him. A few days alone in fasting and prayer was not necessarily what God was calling me to. This was a much longer and deeper undertaking. It was a call to sow my life into the cause I believed in: the Great Commission! This was the cause of transforming nations and cities with the power of God: opening up the spiritual atmosphere and bringing God's kingdom into communities, gathering in the harvest of my Lord who had laid down his life for me and the lost multitudes in the world.

I also began to realize why the Church, as it is today, is actually weak and entangled in the sin, ways, and values of the world. Most of us react to situations in exactly the same way the world does. Many of the things that are so dear to us, while good in themselves, end up hindering our very obedience to God. Where we should be expecting to lay down our lives for our faith, we flinch from it because it is simply inconceivable to us. We want to transform our communities for Jesus, but we are part of the very fabric of darkness we want to see broken and get set free from.

> If we are going to make a real difference, we are going to have to rise above the impediments of our communities and cultures, let go of a lot of things we cherish, and change our priorities and our discipline.

If we are going to make a real difference, we are going to have to rise above the impediments of our communities and cultures. We are going to have to shed a lot of things we cherish. Our priorities will have to change and so will our discipline. But in exchange, we stand to get into a place of confidence with God that opens up a whole new range of godly exploits. This is what the giants of faith experienced, as described in Hebrews 11.

That evening, as I was praying, the Lord said,

> *"This call of separation unto me is not just to you alone. This is the call of the hour for my people worldwide. Surrender and set yourselves apart unto me. I will separate you from your weaknesses. I will make you the people I will use to overturn nations and cities in these last days. I will gather in your loved ones, transform your communities, and bring glory to my name. I want you to tell this to my people everywhere you go."*

By calling us to be surrendered and set apart unto him, the Lord is seeking to take us to levels far beyond what we would be capable of in normal circumstances. We need to go that extra mile if we are to make any meaningful impact on the nations in our generation. Some of these things we truly cannot do for ourselves; we don't even know how. Some weaknesses and shortcomings we are not even aware of, but in the process of being set apart, the Lord will do exceedingly and abundantly above what we can ask or even imagine (Ephesians 3:20).

GROUP DISCUSSION QUESTIONS

General Discussion Questions (for whole group)
1. What is the general teaching we are seeking to grasp in this chapter?

2. What changes do we/you need to make in response to the lesson this week (in actions, mindset, etc)?
3. This chapter mentions the training and focus that both the firemen and the terrorists had to have on 9/11 to carry out their roles. Is there something in your life that you have trained and prepared for with that kind of resolve? If so, what is it? Before now, have you ever viewed your life with God as requiring that kind of intentionality? Why or why not?
4. What are some of the constraints that hold people back from living a life that is completely set apart for God? In what ways do you see the Church entangled in the ways and values of the world?
5. To be set apart, we need a "dynamic encounter with God through which the Lord Himself makes [us] vessels of honor." According to this, what is our part in this process of transformation and what is God's part?

Personal Application Questions (for breakout groups)

1. What did the Lord impress upon your heart as you read this week?
2. In the description of the set apart life given in God's call to John Mulinde, which aspect of the call or of God's promises is most appealing to you? Which is the hardest for you to believe could happen in yourself? Why?
3. The set apart life requires shedding things we cherish and changing our priorities and disciplines. How does that make you feel? Are you ready to set out on this journey?
4. How can we pray for one another to get to the place with God that we are being called to be?

Weekly Prayer Targets:

1. Spend an extended time in prayer this week. First, spend a few moments in silence listening to what God is speaking to your heart. How will you answer his call?
2. Cry out in honesty before God. Ask him to work deeply in your life to do what you cannot do for yourself.

Chapter 6

Set Apart for a Purpose

And he went up on the mountain and called to him those he himself wanted. And they came to him. Then he appointed twelve, that they might be with him and that he might send them out to preach, and to have power to heal sicknesses and to cast out demons..."

Mark 3:13-15

Looking in retrospect at the impact those 19 terrorists had on the world over 10 years ago, I can understand what it means to be set apart for a purpose. These men were set apart for their goal. It was a wicked, demonic goal. They did their task in the space of a few hours, yet the impact continues to shape and shake the world in every area.

Since the 9/11 disaster, a permanent change has occurred in the nations. Every single system all over the world has changed. Our human mindset, media, education, relationships, politics, religions, medical practice, military training, security systems, travel operations, and so much more, have all changed forever.

The 9/11 attacks also had a vast economic and political impact. For the cost of the lives of 19 hijackers and a financial expenditure of around $100,000 ($US), al-Qaeda, the militant Islamic group responsible for the attacks, effected a trillion dollar decrease in the global market within 1 week, the shake-down and eventual collapse of some of the biggest, most enduring financial conglomerates in the world, permanent economic after-shock ripples, and jittery financial markets. It triggered massive increases in military and security expenditure all over the world, which continues to this day.

Why were the terrorists so effective? Nineteen men set themselves apart, surrendered their lives, decided to consecrate themselves for an evil mission, and remained focused on it. These 19 men turned the world upside down for the cause of evil.

They also caused untold damage to the world economy and to families across the world. They believed a lie and used a biblical principle to fulfill Satan's three-fold agenda in the space of a few hours: to steal, kill, and destroy (John 10:10). These 19 men changed the New York City skyline and the world at large forever.

> The church must fully surrender and yield to God in the way he is calling us. Unless we do, we will never have the impact to be able to fulfill God's purpose in the Great Commission in our generation.

Most people don't want to acknowledge that 19 men could adversely affect more than six billion people, or that they forever changed history and humanity because they radically surrendered their lives to their cause.

As Christians, how can we counter such radical behavior? How can we overcome the darkness that is flooding in? We must set ourselves apart. The Church must fully surrender and yield to God in the way he is calling us. Unless we do, we will never have the impact to be able to fulfill God's purpose in the Great Commission in our generation.

Biblical Examples of Lives Fully Surrendered to God

Having been stopped in my tracks by this call to be set apart unto God, I became more and more gripped by it. While I remained deeply concerned about New York City and the terrorist attacks, I was desperate for a deeper understanding of what was unfolding in my spirit. I turned to the Scriptures to see if I could find any reference to the concept of being set apart, and I was not disappointed.

The call to be set apart appears to be God's precondition to major interventions in human affairs. The Bible shows that every time God wanted to bring about a fundamental change in his dealings with human beings, he called out a people or an individual and set them apart for himself.

He called them out of the system they were used to, out of their constraints, their environment, and their comfort zones. He then worked in their lives in such a way that they were totally transformed and able to accomplish things that were previously impossible for them.

Abraham. The story of Abraham was the first to come to mind. Humankind was lost, and God wanted to begin the process of redemption. His plan was to establish one race that he would use to demonstrate his nature and character in such a way that the lost world would eventually choose to return to him. But how could he ensure that the people he would take as his own would not become like the rest of humankind? After all, they would live in the midst of the others! How could he keep his chosen people from adopting the mindset and worldview of the rest of the human race?

God chose to ensure this separation by calling one man out from the rest, setting him apart for his purpose, and then making an infallible covenant with him. That meant that the anchor of the deal was God himself and not man. That man would be able to live above the bondages and constraints of his generation. Thus, Abraham was called out of the culture, traditions, attitudes, and lifestyle of his generation. He was called out so that he could wholeheartedly embrace the full revelation of God's counsel and enable the Lord to fulfill his plan and promises in him.

> *Now the LORD had said to Abram: "Get out of your country, from your family and from your father's house, to a land that I will show you. I will make you a great nation; I will bless you and make your name great; and you shall be a blessing. I will bless those who bless you, and I will curse him who curses you; and in you all the families of the earth shall be blessed."*
>
> Genesis 12:1-3

The people of Abraham's time were descendants of Noah, saved from the flood and survivors by grace, but all of them had sunk into grave depravity that resulted in the confusion of Babel and consequently the great dispersion (Genesis 11:1-9). So God called Abraham out from his family, from his country, his environment, his cultural constraints, and all other types of limitations. God promised to make out of him a new nation, which would be called by God's own name. God told Abraham that through this new nation, he would bless all humankind. In other words, this would be a special nation, a nation set apart for the purpose of redeeming the lost nations of the world.

God needed a new foundation. He needed a people with different values, a different worldview. Through Abraham's obedience in being set apart for God, a channel was made available through which God could reach out to all humankind with the way of salvation.

Joseph. Joseph was another man set apart for God's use to accomplish a divine mission.

> *The blessings of your father have excelled the blessings of my ancestors up to the utmost bound of the everlasting hills: They shall be on the head of Joseph, and on the crown of the head of him who was separate from his brothers.*
> Genesis 49:26

Note the phrase, "separate from his brothers." Deuteronomy 33:16b repeats the same words:

> *Let the blessing come on the head of Joseph, And on the crown of the head of him who was separate from his brothers.*

Joseph was his father's favorite child. As a young boy, God showed Joseph visions of the calling on his life and Joseph shared the visions with his relatives. Unfortunately – or fortunately perhaps – his relatives didn't receive them very well. His father didn't believe him and his brothers became envious. It was an environment in which God's purpose for Joseph's life could not come to pass. Joseph needed to be separated from that environment in order to be prepared for God's calling on his life. He needed to be set apart; in the process, he lost everything he prized and trusted in.

The first thing he lost was the security of his family. He was sold into slavery. He was taken out of his comfort zone, the culture of his family, and the norms he was used to, and placed into a land with a different culture, language, lifestyle, etc. In Egypt, where he was taken, Joseph had to let go of the values and attitudes he had acquired from his family. He had to begin life afresh. The pride of family connections vanished.

Potiphar, an official of Pharaoh the King of Egypt, bought Joseph. Soon Joseph became Potiphar's favorite servant, just as he had been his father's favorite child, and he prospered in Potiphar's house. It was not long, however, before he found himself in prison, by God's appointment. God was taking away Joseph's dependence on his natural abilities, which had enabled him to become Potiphar's favorite. No, the devil didn't cast Joseph into prison; God did!

In prison, Joseph used the spiritual gifts God had given him. He started interpreting dreams and prophesying. Even those gifts, however, didn't immediately get him out of prison. He spent years in jail with his gifts. God wanted him to learn to not even depend on his God-given spiritual gifts.

Finally, after years of God working deeply within Joseph, he was set apart and ready for God's use. He was ready to rule. As Joseph stood before Pharaoh, he had nothing to boast of in himself. Asked how he was able to interpret Pharaoh's dream, Joseph said, "It is not in me; God will give Pharaoh an answer of peace" (Genesis 41:16). All Joseph had at that time was God. No confidence in his human abilities, family connections, or even spiritual gifts.

Years later, Joseph met his family. By that time, though, he was such a different man that they could not change him. Instead, he was in the position to change them, and he did. He was a man set apart for God's use.

Moses. God told Abraham that his descendants would go into slavery for 400 years, but then he would set them free and take them back to the land of Canaan. When the time came for deliverance, God chose a man and set him apart for the task.

Moses was brought up in Pharaoh's palace. He was in line to become Pharaoh himself. He knew everything about Egypt: the lifestyle, attitudes, and worldview. By human standards and in the worldly sense, he was a man destined for greatness.

Moses had a calling on his life to deliver the Israelites and he knew it. The desire to see his people set free was burning in him like a fire. He was full of zeal. In fact, his human zeal made him kill a man in an attempt to deliver his people. However, as long as Moses had so much of Egypt in him, God could not use him. He had to first be set apart from the things he had learned to value, trust, and depend on.

God used the incident of the murder of the Egyptian to get Moses away from Egypt; for 40 years he was alone in the land of Midian as a fugitive. When he went back to stand before Pharaoh as God's vessel, Moses had nothing of Egypt in or about him. He was a changed man, set apart for God. God had now anointed him with authority, not only over Egypt, but also as a shepherd over Israel.

Joshua. For most of the 40 years that Israel wandered in the wilderness, while everyone slept in their tents, Joshua spent his days and nights in the Lord's tent. Whenever Moses went into the tent to speak to the Lord, Joshua was there (Exodus 33:11). When Moses went out to the people, Joshua remained in the tent with the Lord. When Moses went up the mountain to seek God, Joshua accompanied him. He never saw or experienced God like Moses, but he was there. When Moses died, Joshua was God's natural choice of successor. God told him in effect, "Joshua, you who have set yourself apart for me for so long, arise, because I will use you to bring my people into the land I've promised them."

Daniel and the Three Hebrews. Daniel, Meshach, Shadrach, and Abednego were among the captives carried away from Judah by Nebuchadnezzar, the King of Babylon. Although a heathen, the Babylonian king understood the concept of being set apart. He commanded that some young men from among the captives, including the four mentioned above, be taken, set apart, and trained in the science and skills of Babylon. They were to be fed on the king's food during their period of training, and after 3 years, were to be presented before the king.

However, the Bible says, "Daniel purposed in his heart that he would not defile himself with the portion of the king's delicacies, nor with the wine which he drank..." (Daniel 1:8). This was true also of the other three Hebrew boys. They refused to adhere to the Babylonian dietary system. Does it mean they were cloistered in a separate place? No. These boys were captives. They did not have much say over the pattern of their lives. They were slaves to do the bidding of their masters.

They were being trained with other witches and wizards of Babylon in the same class. They were learning the Babylonian culture, politics, science, history, and court etiquette. They were in the thick of Babylonian palace intrigues. Yet they chose to set themselves apart for God, believing that God would honor their faith and commitment.

The result was that God used them to challenge the wisdom and mindset of the Babylonians. God gave them authority over the land of their captivity, with Daniel ending up as Prime Minister.

John the Baptist. The Lord showed me that all the people whom He mightily used, both in the Old and New Testaments, were set apart. When God wanted to introduce a new era, a new phase in his dealings with humankind, John the Baptist was set apart to bring about this fundamental change. The Messiah was coming!

John the Baptist was set apart even before he was born. When the time came for him to embark on his ministry, he went into the wilderness, and without any form of advertisement, multitudes went out to hear him and be baptized by him. The people were not attracted to John because he was a refined preacher. Neither did they come because his message was soothing to the ears. The Baptist preached a message of judgment and repentance. He was not even polite in his preaching, as his denouncement of the religious elite as a "brood of vipers" clearly illustrates (see Matthew 3:7).

In the natural there was no reason why anyone would leave the high life of Jerusalem and go and seek out John in the barren wilderness. His secret was that he was a man set apart. Jesus himself said that among all born of women, there had never lived a greater man than John the Baptist (Mathew 11:11).

The Apostles. In his gospel, referring to the Lord Jesus Christ, Mark writes,

> *"And he went up on the mountain and called to him those he himself wanted. And they came to him. Then he appointed twelve, that they might be with him and that he might send them out to preach, and to have power to heal sicknesses and to cast out demons..."*
> Mark 3:13-15

After the Lord had spent a night in prayer, he called his twelve disciples to himself. Note that he did not call them to ministry or to a club, but to himself. The purpose for this call was, first and foremost, that the twelve might be "with him." Later on, they were sent out to preach.

The twelve were all adult men who had jobs, families, and their own lifestyles. The Lord wanted to use them to preach the Gospel, but first they had to be set apart from the rest of the crowds that followed him. That was why he called them to be with him. To respond to this call, they had to forego their lifestyle. They had to discard their attitudes and world view. They could not go wherever they wanted anymore.

After the Lord's death and resurrection, he met them and told them, "Tarry in the city of Jerusalem until you are endued with power from on high" (Luke 24:49). They were now ready to be anointed with power and authority. They were ready to be sent out to preach. According to Acts 4:13, the Apostles had such boldness and authority that the Sanhedrin "took note that these men had been with Jesus."

The Apostle Paul. Paul had a tremendous experience on the road to Damascus (Acts 9). He had a powerful encounter with the Lord, during which he heard the voice of God. A few days later, he was filled with the Holy Spirit and experienced a personal miracle of healing when Ananias laid hands on him. He then began preaching immediately. Paul was filled with the Holy Spirit and began to preach, but the process of being set apart was just beginning.

Paul had studied the Pentateuch thoroughly and so he knew the Scriptures. He had the information to prove that Jesus was indeed the Christ promised in the Old Testament. From Damascus, Paul went to Jerusalem and preached while staying with the Apostles, the leaders of the Church, the men who had been with Jesus physically. He became a disciple of the original disciples who had been with Jesus.

You would have thought that with such a background (ie, spectacular conversion, filled with the Holy Spirit, personal miracle of healing, keeping company with the leaders of the Church), God would have started using Paul immediately. Not quite. God had a purpose and a calling for Paul: to break down the barrier between Jew and Gentile by taking the Gospel to the Gentiles. But first he had to be set apart so that God could work within him deeply. Consequently, just when it appeared as if things were beginning to fall in place, persecution arose and Paul had to leave Jerusalem in a hurry, rejected.

For years after that, Paul was hidden from public view. Nobody knows what he was doing all that time. He surfaced again in Antioch, having been sought out by Barnabas, and he joined the ministry team there. One day as the leaders of the church in Antioch were fasting and ministering to the Lord (these were men with a lifestyle of seeking after God), the Holy Spirit said, "Set apart for me Barnabas and Saul for the work to which I have called them" (Acts 13:2). And so the two men were set apart. I don't know how it was done, but they did it. The leaders then continued seeking God, and much later, Paul and Barnabas went out preaching.

Several years later, Paul wrote to the Galatians that God had led him into the desert of Arabia where he had spent 3 years, alone with God. It was there that he was given the deep revelations he taught. God worked deeply in him. When he came back from there, he was a new man, changed forever. Like Moses, Paul met with God personally. He had an extended encounter with the Lord, during which a deep work was done in his life.

Accepting the Call to Be Set Apart

God had told Abraham that his descendants would go into slavery in a foreign country (Genesis 15:13). To fulfill that prophecy, God set Joseph apart and used him. For a while God will let us get on with the things we set ourselves to do, but there will come a time when he will say, "Come apart and be separate. You've seen that I am real. You've proven my faithfulness. I have given you a calling. But now come apart and I will you show how to make things happen my way. Let me do a work in you and then I will use you in the nations."

Beloved, when God sets you apart for a season and works deeply in you, you come out totally different from those who live by the norm. Your heart is different, your rules are different, and your worldview is different. You don't fear what they fear. What they yearn for has no appeal to you. What they esteem is detestable to you. You are different.

> When God sets you apart and works deeply within you, you become totally different from those around you. Your heart is different, the rules you live by are different, and your worldview is different.

If we are going to make an impact, we have got to reach that moment when we make the decision to set ourselves apart for God so that he may work in our lives that which we cannot work in ourselves. That he may make us what we cannot make ourselves. God will then separate us from things that we cannot separate ourselves from and will be able to use us for his glory.

GROUP DISCUSSION QUESTIONS

General Discussion Questions (for whole group)
1. What is the general teaching we are seeking to grasp in this chapter?
2. What changes do we/you need to make in response to the lesson this week (in actions, mindset, etc)?
3. What new insights did you gain into the lives of these familiar Bible heroes? Which did you relate to the most and why?
4. In our culture, what things have we learned to value, trust, and depend on that God needs to set us apart from?

Personal Application Questions (for breakout groups)
1. What did the Lord impress upon your heart as you read this week?
2. In each of the Biblical heroes we read about this week, God called out individuals and set them apart for himself. What is he calling you out of? What are your constraints, limitations, environments, and comfort zones?
3. As you look back on your life, in what ways have you seen God already doing this work?
4. In each of these examples, God called the individual to come away and be with him. What time in your schedule have you set apart to be with God? What aspects of your lifestyle will you have to change or forego?
5. How can we pray for one another as we seek to live a lifestyle of surrender and being set apart to God?

Weekly Prayer Targets:
1. Ask God to begin the work of setting you apart. Ask him to separate you from the things that you cannot separate yourself from. Confess the ways you have tried to change yourself.
2. How far would you like to experience God? Ask Him to make you willing to be willing to be all He intended you to be.

Chapter 7

Nazirites

Nazarite/Nazirite = Combined, these two Hebrew words speak of "being set apart, purified, being made to reflect the glory of God, raised above the norm and given authority over the nation."

Following the terrorist attacks, I couldn't leave America for about a week because all the airports were closed. When I finally managed to travel, I went to Austria, where I continued seeking God, asking Him to teach me more. One morning, while I was reading the Bible, the Lord brought to my attention the word "Nazirite." It is a word that does not occur very often in the Bible, and until that time I thought I knew everything about it.

I looked it up in the Bible package on my computer to see what it really means. I found out that the word is spelled in one of two ways: Nazarite (with an "a") or Nazirite (with an "i"). This is because the word has two Hebrew roots. One is the Hebrew root word Nazir (from which "Nazirite" comes), which means "set apart for God, sanctified, consecrated to reflect God's glory." In essence, *Nazir* means "removed from common standards in order to meet the standard of God." The second Hebrew root word is Nazar (from which we get the word "Nazarite"), which has a similar meaning: "elevated above others, set apart, given authority over the land." Combined, the two Hebrew words speak of "being set apart, purified, being made to reflect the glory of God, raised above the norm and given authority over the nation."

Through my study I discovered that the Nazirites in the Bible came to the forefront when the nation of Israel or individuals encountered situations that were beyond their human ability to deal with, situations that were so impossible that they could not handle them on their own. During such times, people took vows to set themselves apart for God, to live as Nazirites for a time.

Three Categories of Nazirites

There were three categories of Nazirites. The first comprised people who, out of their own free will, set themselves apart for a season. These were temporary Nazirites. The second category includes those who were made Nazirites by other people; for example, Samuel was made a Nazirite by his mother, Hannah. In the last category were Nazirites who were chosen by God, not self-chosen or chosen by parents, but chosen by God himself. They were born Nazirites and had to live as such all of their lives. Examples of this type of Nazirite are John the Baptist and Samson, whom God set apart from before they were born. Much higher discipline was required of such people, and they usually had great impact.

The Lord Jesus spoke of eunuchs (see Matthew 19). He said that some were born eunuchs, others were made eunuchs, and others chose to be eunuchs for the kingdom of God. Eunuchs were people who were separated from others in order to serve certain purposes. For example, they did not marry like everyone else. Eunuchs lived the principles of the Nazirite lifestyle.

People who became temporary Nazirites did so for various reasons. We see examples of this in the Acts of the Apostles. Some were motivated by zeal for God, while others who were seeking a solution to insurmountable problems embarked on a period of separation to seek God and draw close to him. Permanent Nazirites remained that way mainly because of the call of God on their lives.

The Nazirite Lifestyle

People who lived as Nazirites had to take vows to observe certain rules and regulations. One of those rules was that they had to cut off their hair at the beginning of the period of separation and were not allowed to cut it again until it ended, regardless of how long their hair grew. They also vowed not to drink anything intoxicating or to touch anything dead or ritually unclean.

Each of the rules the Nazirites observed had a spiritual implication. For example, by abstaining from alcoholic drinks, the Nazirites were implying that nothing else apart from God would control their lives. Determining not to touch or eat anything unclean was a way of reiterating their total resolve to live a holy life of obedience to God.

Understandably, Nazirites had to exercise a great deal of surrender and self-denial. They couldn't live like everyone else. They weren't free to do a lot of things. It sounds almost like hardship, but the result was that they experienced and brought about great spiritual authority and brought forth great deliverances to the people of God.

Biblical Examples of Nazirites

Samson. Judges 13:1-9 contains the record of the birth of Samson at a time when the nation of Israel was in captivity to the Philistines because of their sins. It was in fact God who had handed them over to their enemies. For 40 years, they were tormented politically, physically, and economically, with no ability to set themselves free.

There are times when we are in bondage because of our own sin, foolishness, wickedness, weakness, or carelessness. At other times, we find ourselves bound by circumstances beyond our control. For example, the wickedness in our own generation can cause many limitations to our faith, to our understanding of spiritual things, and to our understanding of God. It can also cause us to be unable to use the power and tools of God. These are things God has given us – our faith and understanding – to help us fight when we are bound. There are many times when we may not know that we are bound and then we can't even seem to fight against it. Even if we start realizing that we are bound, we're not even sure how to overcome what is considered normal in our day and time.

God sent an angel to a barren woman, Manoah's wife, a victim of the prevailing judgment on the nation, telling her that she had been chosen by God to give birth to a child who would deliver Israel. But the angel gave her a warning:

> *Now therefore, please be careful not to drink wine or similar drink, and not to eat anything unclean. For behold, you shall conceive and bear a son. And no razor shall come upon his head, for the child shall be a Nazirite to God from the womb; and he shall begin to deliver Israel out of the hand of the Philistines.*
>
> Judges 13:4-5

God needed a Nazirite, someone who had been set apart, to deliver Israel. This wasn't a task to be undertaken by just any person. It needed someone consecrated, sold out to God. Samson was set apart from birth.

Samuel. Samuel was consecrated as a Nazirite by his mother. When Hannah asked God for Samuel, she made a vow:

> *O Lord of hosts, if you will indeed look on the affliction of your maidservant and remember me, and not forget your maidservant, but will give your maidservant a male child, then I will give him to the Lord all the days of his life, and no razor shall come upon his head.*
>
> 1 Samuel 1:11

The vows Hannah made were Nazirite vows. God honored Hannah's vows and so Samuel was born a Nazirite. And yes, he did reflect the glory of God. People saw God in him; he had authority over the nation. Although he lived in a generation that the Bible tells us was very wicked, the boy Samuel ministered before God (1 Samuel 3:1). He was a Nazirite, set apart from the rest.

John the Baptist. John the Baptist was a Nazirite. Before he was born, the angel told his father Zechariah that he would be set apart for God, tasting nothing intoxicating and being filled with the Holy Spirit from birth (Luke 1:11-15).

The Apostle Paul. The Apostle Paul took vows to live as a temporary Nazirite at least twice (Acts 18:18, 21:23-26). When things got tough for Paul in his ministry, he made a vow and took time off to set himself apart. It is no wonder that God used him so mightily.

The Nazirite Principle

In John 17, Jesus said, "I was sanctified; I was set apart so that you could be set apart" (John 17:19) and Paul said, "You were given the Holy Spirit so that you could be sanctified, so that you could be set apart" (Ephesians 1:13). The Bible tells us over and over again that if we love the world, if we follow the ways of the world, we are at enmity with God, that the love of God is not in us (Romans 8:5-8).

> We are called to be set apart unto God. Our lives belong to him; we were purchased by his blood.

These scriptures help us realize that we are called to be set apart unto God. Our lives belong to him; we were purchased by his blood.

Giving our lives to God is the minimum requirement of what it means for us to be Christian (1 Peter 2:9; 1 Corinthians 6:20; Luke 10:27).

However, people lose sight of the command to give themselves fully to God. When they lose sight of the call to be set apart, they begin to cast off restraint. That is when they begin to become careless. They start taking on the thinking of the world, taking on the standards of the world, taking on the ways of the world, and they begin to find themselves disconnected from the power, life, wisdom, and ways of God. They wonder why they are not experiencing breakthroughs and they don't see how to go forward.

They begin to lose the inheritance, the gifts, and the fullness of what Christ has offered us, and then they wonder, "Why don't I have the power to break through? Why don't I have the power to accomplish this?" The message of living a life set apart to God needs to be held up in the Church once again so the Church can come into the fullness of the position and stature it once held. This will enable the Church to do the work God has called it to do in the nations.

We Must Change

As we see the state of things in the nations these days, the level of darkness that is pushing harder and harder against us, the level of compromise that is being pushed upon us, and even the mindsets that are being thrust upon us, we realize that opposition to godliness, to being solely given to the Lord, is becoming stronger. It's almost like Christians are being rejected by society, ostracized, and looked down upon.

We can see the way things are going in the world: the way people are beginning to give themselves more and more to darkness, the increasing rejection of Christ and his ways, and the diminishing importance of the Word of God, the ways of God, and the thinking of God. We see the compromise that is coming in the world and the way that it is just growing stronger and stronger, as well as the way that it's coming into the family and even into the Church.

Giving ourselves solely to the Lord, living and holding up his values, is even being ridiculed in our day and time; it's being mocked in our schools and workplaces, in our public sectors and public squares. People are being squeezed and pressured so hard to compromise by the world and its system that if you do not make a firm resolve to set yourself apart, you will be captured by the pressure that is out there in our day and time.

The world system will begin to push against you so hard that you will find if you do not clearly give yourself to the Lord, allowing him to do this work in your life, the pressure that is out there will build. It will increase year after year until you find yourself being caught and swept away with that tide of compromise and not even know it. Therefore, maintaining the integrity and fidelity of the Lord is a critical decision for the Church today.

The Lord has been showing me by his grace how much he's holding me in these times and that he will always do so. But God has been sounding an alarm that we must begin to rise up and radically abandon our lives to him. This is the only way we are going to be able to break through the darkness that is coming at our people and our cities. It is the only way that we are going to be able to withstand the

> God has been sounding an alarm that we must begin to rise up and radically abandon our lives to him.

intensity of the forces that are coming, the rapid ways in which things in the spiritual realm are changing. When God sounds a warning that we had better move from one point to another and we resist and we keep claiming, "It's okay, his grace will be there to hold us," then we will be caught unawares and ill-equipped to face the strongholds, pushes, and pressures that we will be facing.

As long as we are not where God wants us to be in our walk with him, we cannot move forward. So many Christians are suffering in their bodies, finances, relationships, etc. Whole churches and even nations are in bondage to confusion, fear, and other forms of oppression. There are limitations everywhere. We have prayed with no results. We have asked God to remove bad leaders from our governments, but he hasn't. We know what we want to see happen and we ask God to bring these things about, but he seems unreachable. Some of us are even questioning whether prayer works anymore.

Beloved, God is just as ready to answer our prayers today as he has always been. There is power in prayer and, in this ministry, we have always emphasized prayer. I can tell you, though, that there is a place where prayers alone do not avail. During the Old Testament days, people prayed in times of trouble, but that wasn't all. They also gave offerings. There were times when only sacrifices brought results. Today, we do not have to offer physical blood sacrifices but the principle remains the same. If we want to see results, we have to offer our lives as living sacrifices (Romans 12:1), to set ourselves apart for God. There is no other way around this.

> If we want to see results, we have to offer our lives as living sacrifices to set ourselves apart for God.

I believe God is telling us in and through the troubles we are encountering that we aren't where we ought to be. I believe that all the money and effort we are investing into impacting society and the meager harvest we are seeing from that investment is demonstrating that we are not where we need to be. Not all the problems we go through are brought by the devil. God directly permits some of them so that he can get our attention and make us understand how much we need him.

The call of the hour is to be set apart unto God, to radically abandon our lives to him so that he may begin to do a work in us. To begin to separate us from the darkness of our day and time, and to bring us into a position in him that we could never bring ourselves into. We can then begin to do the work we were called to do. He will begin to use us as vessels through which his Spirit and his life may flow to impact societies and bring about what is prophesied in scripture: that great harvest, the great revivals.

We have looked at the call to be set apart; now we will look at the obstacles that keep us from abandoning the whole of our lives and our hearts to Jesus Christ.

GROUP DISCUSSION QUESTIONS

General Discussion Questions (for whole group)
1. What is the general teaching we are seeking to grasp in this chapter?
2. What changes do we/you need to make in response to the lesson this week (in actions, mindset, etc)?
3. How would you define a Nazirite? What are some of the characteristics of a Nazirite vow? What would a Nazirite look like today?

4. Have you known someone who lived a life different from the norm in his or her culture for a specific purpose? Explain.
5. In Bible times, when people were seeking a solution to insurmountable problems they often took a Nazirite vow to seek God and draw near to him. What are some of the insurmountable problems facing the world today?
6. We are commanded to give ourselves fully to God. When we forget this command, we begin to cast off restraint. In what ways Do you see Christians becoming careless, casting off restraint, lowering the standards of God, and taking on the ways and standards of the world?
7. As it says above, "The call of the hour is to be set apart unto God, to radically abandon our lives to him so that he may begin to do a work in us." John the Baptist, Samson, Samuel, and Paul had a radical lifestyle in their day and time. What does radical abandon look like in our day and time?
8. Spend time sharing what you journaled this week (see below, Weekly Prayer Targets).

Personal Application Questions (for breakout groups)

1. What did the Lord impress upon your heart as you read this week?
2. In what ways have you become careless, cast off restraint, lowered God's standards, and/or taken on the ways and standards of the world?
3. Is the Lord calling you into a Nazarite walk? What does it look like? What are the terms the Lord has given you for this walk?
4. How can we pray for one another as we begin this set apart/ Nazarite journey?

Weekly Prayer Targets:

1. Ask God to bring you into the position in him that you could never bring yourself into so that you are ready to do walk the set apart life that he is calling you into.
2. Ask God to use you as a vessel through which his Spirit may flow.
3. This week, spend some time journaling what you have heard God saying to you through this second section of *The Wake-Up Call*. What is God's call for your life? What is your response? Be prepared to share during your group meeting time.

Section 3

What Is Holding Us Back?

Chapter 8

The Idols of Our Hearts

Now some of the elders of Israel came to me and sat before me.
And the word of the LORD came to me, saying, "Son of man, these
men have set up their idols in their hearts, and put before them
that which causes them to stumble into iniquity. Should I let myself
be inquired of at all by them? Therefore speak to them, and say
to them, 'Thus says the Lord GOD: "Everyone of the house of Israel
who sets up his idols in his heart, and puts before him what causes
him to stumble into iniquity, and then comes to the prophet, I the
LORD will answer him who comes, according to the multitude of his
idols."'

Ezekiel 14:1-4

I mentioned earlier that when the Lord first spoke to me about being
set apart and the surrendered life, I thought he wanted me to take
time out for a fast. However, as he led me to look at the examples of
the New York City firefighters and of the terrorists from the 9/11
disaster, and as he revealed the entire concept of being set apart
through the biblical examples we just examined, I realized that it was
not that easy.

The call is to a long journey, to a lifestyle of total consecration. I was
willing to start out on this journey, but could not actually put my
finger on how to begin. So I asked the Lord. I prayed for guidance and
revelation. The answer came in words I least expected: "Son, with all
sincerity, would you say that you are being your best for me in your
life?"

I hope, dear reader, that you notice the strangeness of this question.
He did not say, "Are you *doing* your best for me?" but "Are you *being*
your best for me?"

I immediately understood that the Lord was focusing on how I live
my life for him on a daily basis, not on what I do for him in ministry.

In a flash, four different areas sprang into my mind in which I knew clearly I was not being my best for God. These are areas I had talked to God about several times in the past. I had promised him and myself many times that I would get my act together, yet, for some reason, I had kept postponing taking action. I knew deep in my heart that if I really determined to deal with them, I had the ability to do so. It was perfectly possible. For some reason, though, I kept putting that decision off. Now, however, the moment of truth had come and I had to be sincere with myself and with my God.

I immediately responded by beginning to repent and confess my failure, promising to start dealing with the issues right away, but the Lord cut me short. He said, "Write down all those areas that you know you are holding back from me."

I felt my blood rush to my face and anger rising. "Why should I write down four very distinct things I could name without having to see them on paper?" Nevertheless, I obeyed and wrote them down. As I did so, something else sprang to my mind, which I added to my list as a fifth area. Immediately, another also came up, then another, and yet another. My list then grew quite rapidly until there were 16 items on it. I was shocked! "Oh my God, all these are areas I am holding back from you in one way or another!" I knew I was perfectly able to move all the way, and could have done so any time I chose, but somehow I had always held back.

"So why do you hold back?" the clear voice of the Holy Spirit asked me.

Yes, why? Why did I hold back from that which I knew was the best for me? Why did I hold back from that which I desired so much inwardly? I knew without a doubt that given a chance, I would not choose any other way than the way of the Lord, yet as I lived my life in the free choice that the Lord allows me daily, this is not what I had done. Instead, I chose the opposite and kept promising myself that tomorrow I would change for the better.

It dawned on me that this was the measure of the love for God that I had in my heart. Although I always said that I loved the Lord with all my heart, I was clearly being shown that my love was half-hearted, divided, and given grudgingly.

The Lord then led me to write down all the excuses I normally use to keep me from being what I know I could be in the fullness of God.

I felt so silly because all the excuses suddenly appeared hollow and empty. How could I ever have allowed such foolishness to blind me?

The Lord showed me that behind each excuse was the real reason why I could not be what I desired to be in him. I was led to examine myself and find out why such silly and unconvincing excuses have always satisfied my heart into living with less, when I could have the whole counsel of God. As I slowly listed these, the Spirit said to me,

> There are things you will never achieve in your life until you remove the idols from your heart.

> *"Now you are touching the idols of your heart. These are the things that you love and regard more highly than you love and regard me: the ones you honor above me, in the same way that Eli honored his sons above me (1 Samuel 3:1-4:22). When they demand your attention, it does not matter that you know my will; you will always find a way of obeying them instead of me. This is what keeps you from being the man I want you to be for me. Deep inside you also desire and crave the same, yet you will always stop before you get there unless you overcome. There are things you will never achieve in your life until you remove those idols from your heart. I, the Lord, hate idolatry."*

I was reminded of Ezekiel 14:1-4:

> *Now some of the elders of Israel came to me and sat before me. And the word of the LORD came to me, saying, "Son of man, these men have set up their idols in their hearts, and put before them that which causes them to stumble into iniquity. Should I let myself be inquired of at all by them? Therefore speak to them, and say to them, 'Thus says the Lord GOD: 'Everyone of the house of Israel who sets up his idols in his heart, and puts before him what causes him to stumble into iniquity, and then comes to the prophet, I the LORD will answer him who comes, according to the multitude of his idols.'"*

The Idols of Our Heart

I saw a vision of a man who had hooks sticking out of his back. The enemy was able to throw ropes into these hooks. The ropes were long and allowed the man a lot of freedom, so he appeared to be able to do a lot for God.

However, whenever he was inspired to go all the way for God, he would move forward but he could only go as far as the ropes would allow. When they were fully stretched, he would be restrained. No matter how much he tried, he could not go further than permitted by the ropes hooked to his back.

The Lord showed me that this is what happens to us when we entertain idols in our lives. The idols act as hooks in our backs. The enemy just has to throw his ropes into them and we are restrained. We may seem to be able to do a lot of things, but any time we try to go beyond what the system around us permits, we are immediately restrained. We end up doing much in our own eyes, but only producing results possible within human limitations.

Many have accepted this as the fullness of their ministry. The Great Commission is about discipling whole nations for Christ, but most ministries have given up this dream for a much smaller one of only looking at how much they can achieve as single ministries. However, with the challenges posed by this changing world, God knows the futility of ministry with such a limited view. This is why he calls us be set apart unto him. If we allow him, he will work deeply in our lives to separate us from the things that we cannot separate ourselves from. He will do in us what we cannot do ourselves.

There are some things holding us back that are so deep in us that we don't even recognize them for what they are: hooks of darkness! We never confess them. We have never even thought of dealing with them. But if we are set apart to God, he will reveal them, deal with them, and separate us from them. This will in turn make us into vessels of honor in the hands of the Master.

> Anything that competes with God for the love and control of our hearts is an idol.

Beloved, anything that competes with God for the love and control of our hearts is an idol. It does not always have to be some big ugly thing. Most of the time, our idols are innocent excuses, valid reasons, or harmless amusements. They do have one thing in common, however: they will always provide us with a "good excuse" for failing to live up to the requirements of God.

*Therefore, to him who knows to do good and does not do it, to him
it is sin.*

James 4:17

God is grieved and saddened by the idols we put before him in our
hearts. These idols cause us to stumble and fall. They limit us. We
may want to go all the way with God, but the idols in our hearts cause
us to fail. However innocent they may appear, they are responsible
for our failing to excel in God and for falling short of what we ourselves would love to be for him.

This is not to say that our performance before God is purely dependent on our ability alone. I want to contrast the lives of two men in
the Bible to show how God's grace is demonstrated to a man who is
set apart to him as opposed to one who is not.

David and Saul

David and Saul are men whose beginnings and experiences are
similar in many ways, and yet their ends could not be more different.
Both of them came from families of little worldly significance until
God exalted the two men. Both of them were keepers of animals.
Both were sought out and found by the same man, Samuel. Both were
anointed to become king by the same prophet. Both not only became
king, but also a prophet. During their reigns, both of them sinned
against God. Both of them are on record as having confessed their
sin, or somehow having sought restoration.

But...! God forgave one and rejected the other. David was able to find
restoration and finally died in the Lord, while Saul deteriorated so
much that he became a demoniac craving after innocent life. He died
having fallen so far away that he had to seek the counsel of a witch to
find out the will of God.

What was the difference between these two generals of God?

David came from a background of being set apart for God right from
the beginning. Even before he was anointed for kingship, Samuel reported, "The LORD has sought for himself a man after his own heart"
(1 Samuel 13:14). He is one of the men of God we see in the Scriptures who was indeed set apart for God. He had his heart set on God.

Saul was also a man who loved the Lord and fought many battles in

God's name. He did many wonderful things for Israel. However, unlike David, Saul's heart was set on pleasing the people and maintaining a good image before them. The fact that it was God who had actually made him king didn't matter very much to him. For the people's sake, he readily went against God's wishes.

The first instance we see this is in 1 Samuel 13:1-14, which describes how Saul prepared for war with the understanding that Samuel would join him on the seventh day and offer a sacrifice to God before the army went out to fight. However, before Samuel arrived, the Philistine armies gathered, setting up their camp opposite the Jews. When they saw the large numbers of Philistines, the men of Israel lost heart and started to hide in caves, thickets, rocks, and pits. Some even crossed the Jordan to the lands of Gad and Gilead.

When Saul saw that his men were deserting him, everything within him began to panic. He decided that rather than wait for Samuel any longer, he would perform the priestly duty of offering the sacrifice, even though that was not his responsibility. Just after he had done so, Samuel appeared and inquired what the King had done. Saul's answer is very telling: "When I saw that the people were scattered from me" (1 Samuel 13:11). Judgment was prompt and immediate: the kingship would not be passed on to his descendants.

The Lord later sent Saul on a mission to attack and totally destroy the Amalekites because of the evil they had committed against the people of Israel (1 Samuel 15:2-3). He was not to leave a single one of them alive, but Saul did not do exactly as the Lord had commanded. The Bible tells us that Saul and the people were "unwilling" to utterly destroy everything as the Lord had commanded (1 Samuel 15:9). They were just unwilling!

On returning from battle, Saul felt so good at having carried out a successful mission for God that he even went to Carmel and erected a monument to himself as a memorial. While he was celebrating the Lord's victory through him, God in heaven was grieving over him for rejecting his word and instead choosing to do his own bidding (1 Samuel 15:10-12).

Beloved, this scenario is being repeated daily in our churches today. Many of God's servants are unconcerned about whether they are carrying out God's instructions in full obedience. They do their own thing in the name of the Lord while congratulating themselves for having obeyed God. People may look at our lives outwardly and say, "Oh, great man (or woman) of God, obedient to God and wholly following him," but inside we know that we are living in disobedience. We should not allow the applause of people to deceive us into celebrating what we know is our disobedience as if it were obedience.

People only see what is on the surface, but we know what is going on inside. We can tell when we are not pleasing God. Heaven may be grieving over our lives, while on earth we are celebrated as wonderful, obedient giants of God. "That pastor is a mighty man of God," the people say. "See how his church is so full of life and fire!" In heaven, God is saying, "I regret that I ever sent that man to start that congregation. He is living in disobedience. He is not doing what I sent him to do. He is running the work according to his own plans. All he cares about is what people think of him and not my purpose for the work I have placed in his hands."

That was exactly the case with King Saul. When he met Samuel, he proudly reported that he had done what the Lord had sent him to do: destroyed the Amalekites and their belongings, including their animals. Samuel then asked about the bleating of sheep and lowing of cattle he was hearing. Saul answered, "Oh, they are from the Amalekites. You know the people spared the best sheep and oxen to sacrifice to the Lord your God, and the rest we have utterly destroyed" (1 Samuel 15:15). Surely Samuel should be happy; after all, the people were so thoughtful! But were they?

Notice how Saul brought "the people" into the conversation. God's instructions to him were very clear. He had chosen not to do as God had required, but here he was saying it was the people who had acted contrary to God's word. When Samuel suggested to him that he had not obeyed the Lord, Saul was unrepentant. Why had he taken the spoil and spared Agag the Amalekite king? Saul argued that he had fully obeyed the Lord. He had gone on the mission on which God had sent him. The only slight difference was that the people had insisted on taking back the best of the sheep and oxen.

Saul would not take the blame. He saw the whole thing as really "no big deal." "Come on, Samuel, it's not really that bad! We only saved the best to sacrifice to your God. Come on, look at it from our perspective. See the people's point of view. After all, generally speaking, we really did obey God, didn't we? We destroyed the Amalekites!"

There is much service of this kind to our God today. I pray that we would all examine ourselves lest we finish in the same way as Saul.

A careful examination of Saul's life will show us that he had a problem that Samuel actually called idolatry. In 1 Samuel 13:11-12, which describes the offering that he should not have made, Saul explained his action by saying, "When I saw that the people were scattered from me..." In 1 Samuel 15:15, when Samuel confronted Saul about the Amalekite mission, the king replied, "The people spared the best of the sheep and of the oxen to sacrifice to the Lord your God; and the rest we have utterly destroyed." When Samuel accused him of disobedience to the Lord, Saul answered, "But I have obeyed the voice of the Lord and gone on the mission on which the Lord sent me...but the people took the plunder to sacrifice to the Lord" (1 Samuel 15:20-21). Samuel answered Saul,

> *Has the LORD as great delight in burnt offerings and sacrifices, as in obeying the voice of the LORD? Behold, to obey is better than sacrifice, and to heed than the fat of rams. For rebellion is as the sin of witchcraft, and stubbornness is as iniquity and idolatry. Because you have rejected the word of the LORD, He also has rejected you from being king."*
>
> 1 Samuel 15:22-23

Saul replied, "I have sinned, for I have transgressed the commandment of the LORD, and your words: because I feared the people and obeyed their voice" (1 Samuel 15:24). He then requested that Samuel go with him to worship the Lord and make things right, but Samuel refused. Samuel turned to walk away from the King, but Saul grabbed his robe and it tore. At this Samuel prophesied, "The LORD has torn the kingdom of Israel from you today, and has given it to a neighbor of yours, who is better than you" (1 Samuel 15:28).

Immediately, the idol of Saul's heart rose up within him and demanded attention. He said to the prophet, "I have sinned; yet honor me now, please, before the elders of my people and before Israel" (1 Samuel 15:30). There it is again! The people!

Notice Saul's type of repentance. "I have sinned," he said, but then in the next breath he begged for honor because what would the people say? He said, "Honor me now, please, before the people. Yes, I have sinned but don't degrade me. Don't take away my honor. Do not take my peace away."

Do Not Take Away Our Peace. I have been to some churches where the preaching brought conviction to the people and they began to cry out for mercy because of their sin. Then the pastor has said, "Come on! Hallelujah, rejoice! We must rejoice because we are under grace. We are saved by grace and are going to heaven, come what may!"

When the Holy Spirit comes and convicts of sin, there will certainly be grief and people may feel dejected, but that's OK! God is actually working deeply in their lives. It defeats the purpose of conviction when a man of God quenches the Spirit by saying, "Hallelujah! We must not get sad about our spiritual state." In other words, "Quench the conviction, quench the Holy Spirit, please. We need our peace more than anything, even more than God!"

Ease and convenience have become our idols, and many preachers faithfully shepherd God's people into this idolatry. That type of leadership is nothing but enmity to the souls of God's people.

At another time you find the same leader saying, "Let's pray for revival!" What kind of revival will that be without the conviction of the Holy Spirit?

Beloved, if we want to continue playing church, that is OK, but if we want revival, we have got to make a choice. I know most Christians sincerely believe they are living for God, but the question is, how much are we not living for God? And if we are not living for God in certain areas, then for whom are we living?

Can two walk together unless they agree (Amos 3:3)? Will God use us to transform our communities if we cannot even agree with him concerning our own lives?

Self-Esteem. A deeper examination of Saul's character reveals that his idol was really the love of his own reputation and image before the people. This desire for cheap popularity is a very common human weakness. Saul was so obsessed with his image before the people that he would do anything to remain in their high esteem. The reason he offered a sacrifice that he was not qualified to offer was because he could not bear the thought of losing the trust and confidence of the people. He chose to disobey God by allowing the people to do what they wanted in contradiction of God's instruction because he feared losing their favor. He chose to cater to the people's favor rather than to the Lord's!

Worst of all, at the moment of repentance, which calls for humility, Saul demanded to be honored before the people and not forced to lose face before them. It is this same idolatry that led him to resent David for being more popular. He ended up hunting down David to kill him, a mission he pursued for the rest of his life. He disregarded all the signs that showed that God's favor was with David and that David posed no threat to him. Many times he confessed his sin only to return to it again. He slipped further and further from the Lord until he lost the Spirit of God and was possessed by an evil spirit. He later ended up having to consult a witch for guidance because he could no longer hear from God (1 Samuel 28:7-8).

What About Us?

How many of us today disobey God because we don't want to be unpopular? How many times do we perform the same kind of acts of disobedience as Saul because we don't want to antagonize people, willfully holding back from obeying God if we sense that people may not approve? Your life may be a huge scandal as far as God is concerned, even though you retain your position in the church or ministry, but one day down the road it will all come tumbling out into the open.

There was a pastor in England who knew for a long time that God wanted him to move in a particular direction. There were things God wanted him to do and things he was to let go of. I spoke to him some years back and told him that God wanted to use him, but he always excused himself because, "The parish would not allow it. What would the parishioners think? What would people say?" Since the parish employed him, he was worried about what the people would say and feared that they would not move with God. Later, things got so bad in the parish that he had to resign and has since started his own ministry.

Beloved, there are times when we fail God, not because we are incapable of doing right, but because of the people around us and the society we live in. The subtle part of the deception is that in spite of our failures, we are happy to report that we are obeying God! We argue that God understands that we are doing our best; therefore he does not really mind, even when we deliberately choose to act contrary to his commands by honoring people before him.

We do not realize how much our world system has got the better of us. Our world is dictating what we can and cannot do for God. But this is not so much because the world is too powerful for us to resist; rather, it is because there are things we love more than we love the Lord and the world conveniently seems to offer them to us.

Because of this kind of understanding and compromise in today's Church, most of us do not regard the offences of King Saul as particularly grave. We see that in each instance he allowed the right thing to be done, but with some compromise in the details; that does not really matter to us because we too do it every day. Most of us know God has called us to be something in our individual lives and to play an important role in the lives of people in our families, cities, and nations, but in many cases we have failed because of our compromised obedience. This is usually because there are things more important to us than God. It is a sad truth and one that most people will not readily admit, but the fruits of our lives reveal it all.

David

While Saul was obsessed with his image before people, David seemed to care more about his image before God. It is written about him that he was a man after God's heart (1 Samuel 13:14). When the prophet Nathan accused David of sin in the case of Bathsheba, David did not try to play it down or deny it; he began to fast, pray, and seek God. All Israel knew about the great sin he had committed, but he didn't try to hide it. He openly repented. His servants begged him, "Please, King, eat something. Don't keep beating yourself up!" (2 Samuel 12:15-16). But he wouldn't listen to them. He focused on God.

Is the Holy Spirit Really With Us?

God deals with us in seasons and there are times when he tells us, "Let's move on." If we don't move with him at that particular time, we could end up like Saul. Even after the Spirit of the Lord had left Saul, he remained king for years. People saw and treated him as king. They didn't see anything different; nevertheless, God had left him. Not only did the Holy Spirit leave Saul, but a demonic spirit also started tormenting him. People around him wondered what to do and eventually brought David to minister to him. Even that, however, could not restore him. He sank deeper and deeper under satanic oppression.

Many false doctrines come into the Church because people reach the same point as Saul. At one particular point in time, perhaps God speaks to individuals instructing them to change, but they fail to act and eventually reach the place where they want to walk in the power of God but they cannot. They then try to conjure up something to prove that God is still with them. On the outside they still appear every inch a genuine Christian. Once in a while they attend a conference and experience some kind of relief, but they are not completely restored. That seed of bondage remains in their lives. In the end they begin to criticize anointed and functional ministries, finding fault with everything to try to justify themselves.

Saul reached that place of no longer moving under the anointing. He attempted to destroy those with the anointing (David) because he did not deal with his problem. He rejected God's counsel and ended up in a place where God would not speak to him anymore.

> *If you had responded to my rebuke, I would have poured out my heart to you and made my thoughts known to you. But since you rejected me when I called and no one gave heed when I stretched out my hand, since you ignored all my advice and would not accept my rebuke, I in turn will laugh at your disaster; I will mock when calamity overtakes you – when calamity overtakes you like a storm, when disaster sweeps over you like a whirlwind, when distress and trouble overwhelm you. Then they will call to me but I will not answer; they will look for me but will not find me.*
>
> Proverbs 1:23-28

Beloved, let us not be deceived. God cannot be mocked. What we sow we shall reap. Saul was anointed king of God's people, a prophet used by God, and yet he ended up seeking a witch to tell him what God was saying. Even the witch asked him, "What do you want from me?" The time will come when the world will tell the Church, "What are you believers seeking from us? How come you are coming to us for help?"

GROUP DISCUSSION QUESTIONS

General Discussion Questions (for whole group)
1. What is the general teaching we are seeking to grasp in this chapter?
2. What changes do we/you need to make in response to the lesson this week (in actions, mindset, etc)?

3. What does God desire to reveal when we make excuses and hold back regarding our wholehearted service to Him?
4. What is the difference between "doing" your best and "being" your best?
5. Why did God forgive and restore David yet reject Saul? What was exposed as the primary motive in each man's heart?
6. Can you see similar scenarios being repeated in our churches today? Explain.
7. Examine the difference between the worldly sorrow of Saul and the godly sorrow and repentance of David.
8. What excuses and arguments did Saul make when Samuel confronted him regarding his disobedience?
9. How did David respond to Nathan when his disobedience was exposed?

Personal Application Questions (for breakout groups)
What did the Lord impress upon your heart as you read this week?
1. Are there areas holding you back from the fullness of God in your life? Share anything the Holy Spirit has revealed that competes with God for the love and control of your heart.
2. Through the examples of Saul and David, we have seen some of the effects of the idols that are in our lives. What are some of the things that "hook" you when you try to go forward with all your heart?
3. Remembering the examples of Saul and David, how do you respond when you are held accountable for your actions?
4. How can we pray for one another as the Lord reveals the idols in our own hearts?

Prayer Targets:
1. Ask God to uncover and reveal any idolatry in your heart as you submit to his examination.
2. Seek God in prayer to lead you by his kindness into repentance and not to resist or quench the work of the Holy Spirit in you.
3. Pray to submit to God's light and allow him to uproot any hidden sins that are causing you an idolatrous heart hiding behind excuses, self-defense, and self-justification.
4. Pray for the Church of Jesus Christ to return to their first love with all of their hearts positioned in full surrender to do His will.

Chapter 9

Procrastination and Distractions

A Word From the Lord to John Mulinde:
"There are men in your country whom I used mightily. Everybody honored my name on their lives. But a time came when I called them away to come back and just be with me because I wanted to take them to the next level. What I had sent them to do at their level had come to an end. They postponed and postponed, but I was very patient with them.

Why did they postpone? They were so busy serving my people, but they had no time to come to me when I called them. A time came when they postponed too long, and the mandate under which they operated came to an end."

As I allowed the Lord to continue to reveal to me the need to surrender myself fully to him and to be set apart, I began to realize that I had only started the journey in my mind; I wasn't getting any further. I asked the Lord why it was so difficult to be set apart for him, and he replied that I should beware of two things: procrastination and distractions.

I immediately understood why procrastination is an enemy of giving our best to the Lord. All of us who are sincere can testify that we have allowed procrastination to mess up our resolve to be serious about the things of God again and again. We make up our mind to spend time seeking God, and when we begin, we experience joy and peace. We are encouraged. As we go on, however, at some point, something crops up, maybe an emergency, a need for ministry, or some other demand. We quickly change our mind and tell God that we will get back to Him later. Would he please excuse us so that we can handle the emergency? Or maybe the Lord reveals something in our life that isn't right, and we tell him that we will deal with it later.

Beloved, when we tell the Lord that we will deal later with the issues he is telling us to deal with now, we cannot continue enjoying our walk with him. The anointing lifts off us. The presence of God goes.

The joy goes. We may even continue seeking the Lord, but as long as that issue is in our lives, our prayers will become cold, dry, and empty. We may have our reasons why we feel we cannot face our sins and get them out of the way once and for all, but as long as we keep saying, "Later, Lord. I will deal with it later!" it is almost as if God also says, "And I will meet you later, too."

> Beloved, when we tell the Lord that we will deal later with the issues he is telling us to deal with now, we cannot continue enjoying our walk with him.

If you are a minister of the gospel, sometimes the Lord may show you he wants you to move from one point to another within a certain period so that you will be prepared for a future ministry engagement. He knows that the people you are to minister to and the events you are to face require a special word from him, and so you need to move to another level, you need to work on your life, you may need to let some things go. You know there is a time limit, and so you begin to plan to work on what God has pointed out to you. But then things happen that distract you and move your focus onto something completely different. You soon realize that you are not on track and you feel a sense of guilt. You say, "Oh God, have mercy. Bear with me. Give me the strength, the grace. Tomorrow, Lord." Sometimes you say, "Lord, starting next week, I will change." It goes on like that until suddenly you realize the engagement is for the following day and you have not allowed God time to work on your life as he had wanted.

You keep the engagement. Outwardly, you are a very faithful minister. The people see a man or woman of God, but they don't know what you are going through on the inside. As you mount the pulpit, you whisper a desperate prayer: "God, I have let you down. Forgive me. But please, Lord, it is not about me. For the sake of your people, stretch forth your hand. Please work. I promise that as soon as I finish this I will start on the journey." Sometimes you stand up there and God does his work nevertheless, and you breathe a sigh of relief: "Thank You, Lord. Where would I be without your loving kindness?"

This does not happen just to gospel ministers. You could be a businessperson, a housewife, or whoever. You know that God is saying, "Move on. I want to use you. I want to change your world through you," and within you, you really want to do it. You know it is the best thing for you. You know that if only you could move to that place in your life, you would be fulfilled. You make a resolution that you are going to obey. But then other things begin clamoring for your attention, too. Pretty soon, you are bargaining with God: "Lord, give me a little more time. I can't get started right now." After a while, you begin to feel that maybe God is grieved. So you stop talking about it for some days. This goes on and on.

It is not that we don't love God. What I am describing is the situation of lives not being wholly yielded. We give, but not all of ourselves. We love, but not wholly. We don't love him with all our heart. In word we say it and sometimes we convince ourselves that we mean what we say, but when we are really honest with ourselves, we find it is not true.

> We are all guilty of postponing the fulfillment of promises we have made to God. We have all at one time or another postponed acts of obedience the Lord has called us to do.

Beloved, God will not let us go forward until we have dealt with the things he is showing us. Just when our devotional prayers are becoming deep and sweet, those issues will come back to our minds, and because we aren't willing to deal with them, our prayers die right there, as if a cold bucket of water is poured over us. Sometimes, we stop praying altogether for a while, or whenever we pray and the issues come to mind, we try to avoid mentioning anything about them.

We are all guilty of postponing the fulfillment of promises we have made to God. We have all at one time or another postponed acts of obedience the Lord has called us to do. The Lord tells us to take a fast, and we say, "Not now, Lord; next month." We actually bargain with the Lord to disobey him: "Lord, I know what your will is. I know that this sin in my life is the reason why I am not doing well, but let me first solve a few problems. I will deal with what you are saying later. Please understand and bear with me, Lord!"

So we keep procrastinating. Sometimes, we postpone acts of obedience for years. Five years after the Lord first called on us to get rid of something wicked in our life, we are still saying, "Later, Lord." In the meantime, we pray, but there are no breakthroughs. We tell God that we love him, but deep in our heart we know we are lying. We may even try to use high-sounding words, maybe the English of the King James Version of the Bible, to try to impress God so he doesn't remind us of the issues. Or we may decide to keep our prayers superficial, avoiding going any deeper in case the issue comes up. In the meantime, we have no fellowship with our God.

To make everything worse, the more we procrastinate, the harder our hearts become. By postponing obeying the Lord, we are quenching the voice of the Holy Spirit, the only voice who can lead us to repentance. As we keep pushing aside the conviction of the Holy Spirit, he too keeps going further and further away. Thank God for his immeasurable patience. He never gives up on us, but how much we must hurt him with our disobedience!

A few years ago I had one of the hardest years in all my years of serving God. Every moment I had I wanted to spend pursuing this journey, asking God questions and seeking to go unto him. Just to stop to do that and to begin to prepare for preaching had been a great sacrifice every time. There were some days when I got distracted or discouraged. I would lay the whole thing down for days, feeling like, "I know I am willing to go back but I have no strength to turn back again." Then one evening, I had promised the Lord to make time for him, wait upon him, and seek the direction he was sending me.

Evening came and I did not want to do it. I did not even feel like praying. So I began to debate with myself, "But Lord, does it have to be this way?"

Here is what the Lord spoke to me:

> *"There are men in your country whom I used mightily. Everybody honored my name on their lives. But a time came when I called them away to come back and just be with me because I wanted to take them to the next level. What I had sent them to do at their level had come to an end. They postponed and postponed, but I was very patient with them.*
>
> *Why did they postpone? They were so busy serving my people, but they had no time to come to me when I called them. A time came when they postponed too long, and the mandate under which they operated came to an end.*
>
> *I have not rejected them. I don't hate them. I miss them. I want to move with them, but I have moved on to the place I called them to be and they stayed there. They are still serving the people, but*

*everybody knows their anointing is no longer what it used to be.
Things have changed."*

Why could they not seek the Lord? They were too busy; the demands
of the people were too many. Today, where are the crowds that
thronged around them? Nowhere. The crowds have dwindled. Something has gone missing. Why? Because God said,

> *"Come away. Come spend time with me like you used to do in the
> beginning. What you did in the beginning, you saw what it bore
> in fruitfulness. You saw how much you were used for that time
> you sowed yourself into my presence. For the time to be there and
> be taught by me. Come again. I will teach you again. I will break
> things in you that you don't have power to change by your own
> self. Then I will launch you into the next phase. I will give you new
> mandate."*

They were too busy. When God said this to me, I cried and cried. I
went to preach that evening in a large church. There were about
2,000 to 3,000 pastors and people from different churches. I began
to share the Word. In the middle of the message, the Lord said to me,
"Remember what I told you about the pastor who could not come
back to me. Look at this crowd. There are so many pastors that I used
in the past, but I am no longer working with them today. They know,
that they know, that they know, that they have lost something." I began to share what I was hearing from the Lord.

Even as I was speaking out, the Spirit of God was speaking to my
heart. He was telling me that the time came when these pastors who
were postponing and postponing and postponing eventually realized that the anointing was gone. It is no longer there. So they began
to fast, to receive the anointing to do things they did in the past, and
this time the fasting is no longer producing the same results. They
began to read the Word in the way they used to read it for ministry,
but it was only a shadow of what it used to be. A time came when
deep inside they knew they were not where they are supposed to be.
They know that he has been calling them for a long time.

The time will come when they want to say, "Here I am Lord." When
God calls you, he is at your side to help you, to walk with you step by
step. When you postpone it too long, he will move to the next stage.
He does not hate you, but he is saying, "Come. Come, I am here."
When you begin to try to seek, to take one step, there is no strength.

And the Spirit was also saying that thesse pastors fast, but they cannot finish the fast; there is no strength. They seek, but they don't go to the end. Even when they purpose to be with God for 3 days, after only 1 day they stop because they cannot continue. Deep inside, they know that this is the best for them, but somehow the strength is too low and the price has become too high. They are living in a state of torment, and every day they think, "Oh God, have mercy on me. Have mercy." And the joy of salvation, the joy of the Lord is no longer there. They are holding on by faith.

God has not rejected them. No! they have missed or are missing their destiny. The joy has gone because every day they are consumed by the thought that those around them can see that the anointing is gone and that it is affecting the people around me them.

When people sit down and talk about what God is doing in the nation of Uganda, sometimes they say, "God used that man. You should have been there. My goodness!" Those who never saw the person might ask, "When did he die?" You say, "No, he is not dead. He is still around. He lives in that place right over there." But what happened? Does God use people, then get tired of them, throw them away, and forget about them? Is that his character? No! So what happened?

There was a time when God said, "Set yourself apart. Remember those days when you sought me? You had nothing. Nobody valued you, so you valued me. You sought me and I made you what you are. But now I am calling you to come back and you are telling me, 'Lord, the people, the ministry. Lord, the invitations, the responsibilities.'" God says, "What? Unbelievable. Who gave the responsibility, the ministry, the people to you? Who gave you revelation? Why don't you come back?" You say, "Lord, just give me a little bit longer. I am coming."

The Lord spoke to me that the reason I wasn't getting started on the journey was because I was procrastinating, promising to begin later. And the reason I was procrastinating was because I wasn't yet really willing to deal with the excuses for my disobedience. I was fearful. He showed me that unless I was ready to commit myself and die to the things holding me back, I would continue postponing the beginning of the journey.

He then reminded me of the numerous times in the past when I had made plans to seek him, but then something else had come up and I had changed my plans. I had changed my focus. On other occasions, I had diverted what I had intended to give to the Lord. I could remember times, for example, when I cancelled my plans to pray because of a visitor.

The Lord showed me that those interruptions, whether genuine or not, were distractions. If I wanted to start on the journey of being set apart, I had to deal with distractions. I had to make a choice. I had to make up my mind, right then. As long as I kept allowing distractions to interrupt my plans, I would never make a start.

GROUP DISCUSSION QUESTIONS

General Discussion Questions (for whole group)
1. What is the general teaching we are seeking to grasp in this chapter?
2. What changes do we/you need to make in response to the lesson this week (in actions, mindset, etc)?
3. What things keep us from being wholly yielded to God despite our heart's desire to do so?
4. What are the long-term effects of procrastination?
5. What forms of distraction are in our lives, and how do they keep us from fully surrendering our lives to God?
6. What do you see today that keeps the Church from its desire to be in the presence of the Lord? How is it affecting the spiritual climate around us?

Personal Application Questions (for breakout groups)
1. What did the Lord impress upon your heart as you read this week?
2. Is there anything that you are holding onto that the Lord has instructed you to get rid of? Why are you delaying letting it go? How are you going to respond?
3. Are you postponing acts of obedience by bargaining with God? What are you going to do with that awareness?
4. Are you resisting a move of God, knowing it has been his heart's desire to take you to a new level of faith? What comes against you specifically?
5. How can we pray for one another as we seek to devoid our lives of the procrastinations and distractions that keep us from obeying the instructions and directions the Lord is giving us?

Weekly Prayer Targets:
1. Pray that the Lord would give you an honest heart to admit the things that are keeping you from seeking after him in full abandonment.
2. Ask God for the strength and resolve to put off the things that have separated you and held you back you from your time with the Lord.
3. Pray for full restoration of your love, zeal, and devotion to God.
4. Pray for wisdom and readiness to keep your appointments with the Lord.

Chapter 10

Prison Gates

In the same way, count yourselves dead to sin but alive to God in Christ Jesus. Therefore do not let sin reign in your mortal body so that you obey its evil desires. Do not offer the parts of your body to sin, as instruments of wickedness, but rather offer yourselves to God, as those who have been brought from death to life; and offer the parts of your body to him as instruments of righteousness. For sin shall not be your master, because you are not under law, but under grace.

Romans 6:11-14

So much compromise and worldliness has been allowed into the Church in this time in history that sin is being permitted to reside in our lives. Because we're comparing ourselves to one another and living our salvation before one another rather than before God, we don't feel convicted that we carry a certain level of sin, and yet the Word says that sin is not to be our master (Romans 6:11-14).

Because we are living our salvation before men and not before God, we begin to settle with and tolerate the sin in our lives. It's either hidden, so we know no one can see it, or we feel we have the same level of sin as others, so we don't feel bad about it. But when we live our salvation before God, we begin to see our sin from God's perspective. We begin to be convicted of our sin and desire to surrender ourselves to God so he can break us free from our sin. We don't do this to become perfect so God will love us; we do it because we love him and we want his life to flow freely through us so our lives reflect his glory.

As I continued to seek the Lord about what he had shown me after the tragedy on 9/11 about the need to be set apart for him, he showed me that it is the sin in our lives that keeps us from fully surrendering ourselves to him. These limitations and bondages that keep us from being set apart fall under three categories: sins that beset, our world system, and the works of the devil. I call these three categories our "prison gates."

As you read this chapter about the prison gates, I encourage you to allow the Lord to plow up your heart and reveal to you those things in your own life that he needs to deal with. The things he reveals to us are those things that hinder us from totally releasing our lives to him; he reveals them to us so that we can be set free and are able to release our lives fully to him so he can set us apart for his purposes. We need to remember that God is not showing us these things and then asking us to deal with them ourselves. Seeing the greatness and the insurmountableness of what is against us is a part of what motivates and compels us to a deeper level of releasing our lives to him and putting our faith in him. Even as you see this, don't run from it; allow the reality of what you are facing to draw you into a deeper place of abandonment and trust in God.

Prison Gate No. 1: Sins That Beset

Hebrews 12:1 says, "Therefore, since we are surrounded by such a great cloud of witnesses, let us throw off everything that hinders and the sin that so easily entangles [the sins that beset], and let us run with perseverance the race marked out for us."

We have a level of control over how far we can be imprisoned by this particular prison gate. It is the one area most Christians will focus on and struggle with when we first hear the call to be surrendered to God.

The sins that so easily entangle are those that have been in our lives for so long that they have become part of us, part of our personalities. Entire portions of our lives are dedicated to them. They are so much a part of our life and how we identify ourselves that we often engage in them daily. These are sins we do not fall into, but rather walk in. They are a part of our thinking, our speech, and our attitudes. We engage in these sins without any feelings of guilt, although at the back of our minds we know they are contrary to God's Word.

These sins aren't always necessarily what we consider to be "big" or scandalous. They could be one of those so-called "harmless" habits, or even omissions – not doing what we know we ought to do. Regardless of whether they are "big" or "small," sins that beset damage our relationship with Christ, stealing joy, peace, and victory from our lives. We cannot hope to go far with the Lord, to walk in his authority and power, when we are habitually and knowingly sinning against him without even feeling any guilt. Sin remains sin whether we con-

The sins that easily beset us usually have their hold on our minds. They have been part of our lives for so long that we have come to accept them as being part of who we are and how we define ourselves.

done it or not, and God, the Holy God, will not work closely with us so long as we walk deliberately in sin.

The sins that easily beset us usually have their hold on our minds. They have been part of our lives for so long that we have come to accept them as being part of who we are and how we define ourselves. We sometimes even become conceited in them; we proudly claim that they are what make us different from others around us! The sins shape and control our attitudes. They have become acceptable and we allow them to have power in our lives, even though we sense that they are displeasing to God.

For example, I know a lot of people with anger who say, "This is just the way I am. I have always been an angry person." To excuse themselves, they may declare that they have always been loud, have always been "passionate." This is something they have come to accept about themselves and they expect those around them to accept it, too.

Another example is people who accept lust as a normal part of their life. Almost every day, whether it's provoked by what they see on television, in printed material, on the computer, or even in person, they have lustful thoughts that are with them continuously. Throughout the day, when their mind is idle and not engaged, they find themselves having lustful thoughts. Lust is with them constantly. They have learned to live with it and have come to believe that this is just who they are.

In this same way, people can have pride, arrogance, fear of man, or excessive behavior. Such things can shape our personalities because we accept them and allow them to be part of who we are and how we speak, think, and behave every single day. For instance, the fear of man can cause us to lie, to disobey God, or to try to please and submit to others rather than to God; it can cause us to run away from the things of God. We just accept this sinful pattern in our life because we've known it for so long and it has become a familiar part of us.

Beloved, God said that we must be set apart from *all* sin if we are to walk with him in the difficult days ahead. Because our cultures, our ways, and our mindsets are filled with so many things that are against God's Word and his ways, many times we don't even recognize the sin in our own lives. The very reason why we abandon our lives to God is so he can bring the light of his Word into our lives; he can begin to strip away the layers of entangling and besetting sin and to free us from their captivity.

There are things you won't even think of because they have been in our culture so long, but as we begin to seek God and abandon our life to him, he will reveal them and begin to show us how to be set free of them. As the light of his Word and his Spirit do the work in our hearts, God will begin to change us, to cleanse us of all sin, and to lead us into a place of full abandonment and surrender to him.

The Bible says that,

> *We know that we have come to know him if we obey his commands. The man who says, "I know him," but does not do what he commands is a liar, and the truth is not in him. But if anyone obeys his word, God's love is truly made complete in him. This is how we know we are in him: Whoever claims to live in him must walk as Jesus did.*
>
> 1 John 2:3-6

and that,

> *Everyone who sins breaks the law; in fact, sin is lawlessness. But you know that he appeared so that he might take away our sins. And in him is no sin. No one who lives in him keeps on sinning. No one who continues to sin has either seen him or known him.*
>
> 1 John 3:4-6

As the Holy Spirit reveals and strips away the sinful thought processes, behavior patterns, etc, our hearts begin to change. We will stop rationalizing and comparing ourselves to other people and justifying our sin, and will begin to release ourselves to God. We will begin to want to obey him, to follow him, and to allow him to do anything he desires to do in us. We will begin to desire a heart of obedience.

God does the work of setting us apart. We do not have to try to become perfect in our own strength; we only need to surrender ourselves to him. As he works to set us apart, he will strip away the layers of sin in our life. He will begin to bring us to a breakthrough where we release the sins that he reveals and come into greater obedience to him. We will begin to desire to obey him, to not want to play mind games any more. We will truly want God to bring us into greater and greater obedience, surrender, and dependence on him.

> God does the work of setting us apart. We do not have to try to become perfect in our own strength; we only need to surrender ourselves to him.

Paul says, "Not that I have already obtained all this, or have already been made perfect, but I press on to take hold of that for which Christ Jesus took hold of me" (Philippians 3:12). Paul did not say, "I just sit in sin and accept it," he said, "I press on toward the goal to win the prize for which God has called me heavenward in Christ Jesus" (Philippians 3:14). He is saying that he has not already obtained everything, but that he presses on to take hold of the plans that Christ Jesus had for his life (Philippians 3:12).

As we surrender ourselves to God, we will not obtain perfection, but we will continue to walk in greater and greater sanctification, and God will continue to draw us deeper into conforming us into his image and doing a greater work in us. When we give ourselves to God, he will give us a heart that no longer finds it acceptable to compromise or rationalize the sin in our lives. We will be willing to go further into obedience and to give ourselves to God so he can do his work in and through us.

Prison Gate No. 2: Our World System

One reason why we are the way we are, why we act the way we do, and why we live the way we live is because of the world that we belong to. When we talk about our world system, many of us immediately think of immorality, drunkenness, and all the usual vices. But I am talking about our world in the sense of the systems around us.

Our world system is the most influential area in our lives. This prison gate has the strongest pull against our ability to be surrendered and set apart. Why? Because it has become what we are used to; it is our norm, our pattern. The system of our world becomes what everybody around us lives in and the way our mindsets function. We have become completely adapted to it. Most of the components of our world seem very harmless; we find comfort in it and want to live in it.

What Makes Up Our World System? Our worlds are made up of harmless things, like our families, relationships, cultures, mindsets, customs, and responsibilities. The various activities that people engage in, including politics, business, education, media, entertainment, relationships, and worship, also help constitute our world system. These are things that we encounter and are involved with every day, and they comprise our activities and the way things normally run and operate in our homes, institutions, and workplaces.

The world system is our way of life. It differs from one nation to another and from one culture to another, but its foundations are the same. And whether we like it or not, it is under one governing body: the ruler of the kingdom of the air (Ephesians 2:2). Its wisdom, its way of thinking, is the wisdom of the world. James 3:15 says that this wisdom "does not come down from heaven but is earthly, unspiritual, of the devil."

This "normal" way of life separates us from God, who says his ways are not our ways and neither are his thoughts our thoughts (Isaiah 55:8-9).

How Does Our World Become a Prison? The parable of the sower gives a clear warning about the danger of being caught up in the world: "Now he who received seed among the thorns is he who hears the word, and the cares of this world and the deceitfulness of riches choke the word, and he becomes unfruitful" (Matthew 13:22, NKJ).

Jesus told us that even though we are in the world, we are not to be of the world (John 17:16). To be of the world is to "belong," to be in the world's power, to be under its influence. Our environment, the people we live among, the traditions and customs of the societies we live in, our cultures – many times, these things that make up our worlds are hindrances to our ability to surrender ourselves totally to the Lord.

You may want to submit yourself fully to everything God wants, but fears begin to rise up. These are the pulls of the world. You may fear that God will lead you outside of the norm. What will people say about me? How will I be perceived? How will this affect the way I live my life, the way I order the world around me? How will that affect my relationships? What will happen with that?

You can feel the pulls of the world and because of the fears that arise, allow them to pull you into the world rather than trusting God and following him wherever he leads.

Romans 12:2 says, "Do not conform any longer to the pattern of this world, but be transformed by the renewing of your mind. Then you will be able to test and approve what God's will is – his good, pleasing and perfect will." The pulls of this world, the people all around us, the norms of society, our culture, our belief systems, all these things put pressure on us. They pressure us to conform, to go along with the status quo. And when we begin to abandon our lives and to set our focus clearly on Jesus Christ, being willing to do anything he says, we sometimes begin to feel like the world is trying to pull us back into the place where it fits our schedule, it orders our lives, it controls what we think and what we do.

There will be times when you know the Lord is calling you into spending your time differently and you will worry, "What will people say? What will happen at my workplace? What will happen with my finances?" This is the pull of the world raising up fear. Every person who is called to surrender will feel the world pulling on them, trying to conform them and keep them locked into the pattern of their world system.

This means that as you abandon your life to God you will have to turn to him and trust him to break the holds the world has on you, the temptations the world has set before you. You can't do this in your power, but as you turn and surrender to God he will begin to break the grip the world has on you. And as God begins to call you out to change your schedule, to walk in a different way, to think in a different way, to live in a different way, you will begin to give yourself fully to him and obey what he says. Even though you feel the power of the world trying to pull you back, you know that your only hope to being fully given to God is to let him break every hold the world has on you.

Many of us have a desire to break through the darkness in our cities and nations, to break through the darkness in our churches and to see a revival and an awakening of God, but we can't even break through the system that is holding all of us captive unless we let God set us free from that system. This makes it vital for us to go against the ways and patterns of our world system and allow God to work in us so that we can be set apart for him.

The Cost of Being Imprisoned in Our World System. We have been called out of our world system and into a new life. We are citizens of heaven. The ways of God are different from the ways of the world (Galatians 2:20, 1 John 2:15-17). The devil knows if we answer that call and live in the ways of God, then we will be outside his grasp. We will live a victorious life. One of the ways he fights us is to convince us, "I'm okay. I'm already born again. I've already got what I want. It doesn't matter. I can live like the rest of the world and think like the rest of the world. God is good and he is pleased with me as long as I confess that he is the Lord." This corrupted wisdom can lull us into darkness, sin, and slumber.

Scripture says, "Not everyone who says, 'Lord, Lord' will enter the kingdom of heaven, but only he who does the will of my Father who is in heaven" (Matthew 7:21). What does that mean? If we conform to the pattern of our world system, if we allow ourselves to think like the world, then we cannot even discern the perfect and good will of God. In such a state and such a lack of clarity, we can take Scripture and turn it around to say whatever we or the world wants to say. The devil knows that, and he does everything in his power to convince us to think like the world and live like the world!

Do you see worldliness coming into the house of the Lord? What does that mean? It means the enemy is taking advantage of us, possibly by leading us into creating our own definition of worldliness. We think that we are walking with the Lord as long as we are not doing those things that we consider "worldly." The deceit is that we are living by standards we have devised rather than by the standards the Lord has set forth for us in his Word. This, too, brings us into a state of darkness, slumber, blindness, and sin.

What I share is real. The enemy has used those good things in our lives to rob us of the fullness of what God has for us. The very "normal" everyday things we are involved in – because they have been corrupted – are responsible for the slumber we talk about and rob us of the impact we should be having in the nations.

The Cost of Living the Set Apart Life. Beloved, there is a price to pay to walk with God. It has always been that way. When God called Abraham, he told him to separate himself apart from his world – his family, his society, and his environment. Abraham could have asked how he and his family were going to survive in a strange land, among strange people. He could have said to God, "At least first show me the land before I move my family there."

There were many reasons why Abraham could have chosen to remain in his world. However, he chose to give up everything that was asked of him, and then to trust and surrender himself to God. Like Abraham, when we decide to trust God and set ourselves apart from our world system, there will be pressures and difficulties, but those who persevere to the end will be saved (Matthew 24:4-13).

Our world system controls our mindsets and attitudes. It works to give power to the sins in our lives. For example, if I am engaging in a particular sin, my circle of friends will help make me comfortable in my prison. They will encourage me to go on sinning because they engage in the same activity or belief system. Through this group support, as we encourage and aid one another, we create a system, a culture of our own. We create an atmosphere around us in which our sins can flow. Within this environment, we develop values, methods of acquiring wealth, rules governing relationships, etc. Eventually, we become so programmed to and by our world system that we no longer even feel concerned with or convicted by the sins that beset us. We have the strength and support of our world. We are anchored to that world; we are part of it and it is part of us.

Because we have been programmed mentally and even physically to fit into our world system, separating ourselves or setting ourselves apart from it isn't easy. It is costly to leave that world. You may have to give up some of your friends. A lot of things may have to change around you. Only people who determine to walk with God will pay the price, but those who seek him and allow him to work in their hearts will overcome.

This is difficult for all of us. At numerous conferences, I have shared with pastors that if they are really going to walk in the power of God they will have to spend time with the Lord. I call them to set aside at least an hour a day to saturate in the Word and an hour a day to draw into his presence in prayer. Many times they tell me, "I can't. I don't have time for that." Who says they can't? Who says they don't have time? Does the system say that or does God say that?

I have even talked with people about the need to establish an altar of prayer in their family and described how that altar of prayer will begin to draw the presence of God, to bring healing to their family, and to push the darkness out of their home. I can share the testimonies of family after family of the work that God has done through a family prayer altar and how the presence of God would even begin to parent their children, but many times they will say, "We can't do that. We can't have that in our home. That won't work in my family." Who says? Their world system.

Many times people will go to a conference and sense the call of God to be set apart. They feel alive and a fire is ignited in their hearts like they've never known in all their lives. They weep before the Lord in deep brokenness and humility, and they start to have a willingness to go all the way with God; they want to give themselves to God in full surrender. But then they go back into their world system, to their families, businesses, churches, etc, and begin to feel the pulls of the world, the system pushing against them.

Everyone faces these pulls and pressures, but the ones who thrive and don't fall back – those who overcome – are those who determine to follow the Lord no matter what they face. Even when they are confronted with their worst fears, when everything within them rises up to say, "Conform! Go back to the way the system wants," they press through and submit to what God asks of them.

> Everyone faces these pulls and pressures, but the ones who thrive and don't fall back – those who overcome – are those who determine to follow the Lord no matter what they face.

Those who persevere are those who begin to see God uproot and change the system like he did to the system of Egypt through Moses. But, sadly, the ones who are intimidated by the system or who cower as the system begins to put pressure on them will see the new life and zeal that was in them begin to deteriorate, dry up, and go away.

This means that we must begin to follow the Lord and be set free from the dictates of the system. We must be willing to turn into the Lord so that he can break the hold the world system tries to have on our minds, our lifestyles, and our hearts.

A Testimony of Our World's Control. A friend of mine who lives in Berlin, Germany, attended a conference in Switzerland that greatly impacted her life. She was charged with so much fire for evangelism that she said to God, "If you will put upon me the anointing and ability to bring people into the kingdom, I am going to witness everywhere." In answer to her prayer, God poured out an anointing on her and she had no doubt that she had received what she desired.

She travelled back home to Berlin full of faith, zeal, and confidence, and immediately asked God for the souls of all the people living in her apartment complex. When she got into the lift to take her luggage up to her apartment, someone else got into the lift as well. The Holy Spirit immediately prompted her to minister to that person. She thought, "Hey, I have hardly got back into my apartment. Not now, Lord." She didn't say a single word.

The next morning she was praying, asking God to send a soul her way. The response was, "How are you going to win people if you aren't going to talk?" She asked for forgiveness and promised to talk next time. After her time of prayer, she met two young boys in the lift. One of them mentioned that his brother was sick. When my friend offered to pray for the sick child, the boys readily agreed even though they were not Christians. She laid hands on them there in the lift, prayed, and the boys left. That evening when she got home, the boys met her and thanked her for her prayer because the sick child had recovered the moment she had prayed. Full of joy, she entered her apartment and prayed, "Lord, I promise that I am going to live for you." A few days later, she met the mother of the boy who had been healed and after she had shared with her, the woman gave her life to Christ.

For about 2 months, my friend talked to a number of people; three of them came to the Lord. Then it started happening: her job slowly began to take her mind away from her desire to serve God. She would come back home too tired to witness. Four months later, her passion and zeal were gone. She still met people who needed help, but somehow she just couldn't bring herself to witness to them.

My friend shared her experience with me, then asked, "Why did God allow me to lose that zeal, passion, and anointing when he knew I really wanted it?" I shared with her that her world system wasn't programmed for the ministry she wanted to do. She had tried to live her life as she had always done, in a "normal" way, even after she had received the new anointing. She had tried to squeeze in this new ministry of God while continuing to live out her life as she had always done, giving time to her job and all the people around her, going on holiday, etc. The result was that her world system squeezed the anointing of God out of her life.

I shared that it would have been best if she had made some life changes and set new priorities when she took on this new mission in her life. Certain things should have been cut out of her life to maintain the anointing. I explained that there was no way she could keep living as she had always lived and still operate under that anointing. She needed to seek God and ask him to set her apart for him; to separate her from her world system in order that she could serve him in the way she desired.

That same lady is a friend of many powerful ministers. She also shared with me a time when she had served for a number of weeks with a man of God from Argentina who is very anointed. Although he is a businessman as well as a great minister, he does not struggle. Signs and wonders follow his ministry. In times of prayer for people's needs, he had asked her to join him in ministering to the people. She had laid hands on people and they had been healed and delivered so easily. Between ministry sessions, she had sat with the man of God, going over Scriptures, worshiping, and rejoicing in the Lord.

When the time came for the man to leave, she had said to him, "It is so bad that you are going away. I love this life of miracles, signs, and wonders. What will I do without you?" The man scolded her for being silly since the Bible says all believers have authority. He had told her just to believe the Word. On her request, he prayed for her to receive anointing.

The following day, she ministered in a small fellowship and the anointing was just as strong as when she had been with the man of God. Whenever she was given opportunity to minister, the Holy Spirit moved with mighty signs and wonders. Things went well for about 6 months and then, nothing. No more miracles. No more fire. No matter what she tried, nothing happened.

When she shared this, I explained that the problem was her world. During the time she had been in fellowship with the man of God, they had sought God together and that was why she had operated under the same anointing as him. As for her, she had not regarded those times of discussion and worship as anything special, just a nice time talking about the things of God. She has not programmed her life to live with God at the level at which she could continually have that anointing.

Breaking Free From the System of the World. Beloved, the way we live our lives is not programmed for revival. If it were, we would have been revived by now. Most of us are captives of our world, obeying the dictates of the routines and systems around us. If we are to allow ourselves to be set apart for God, we need to rethink our priorities.

> The way we live our lives is not programmed for revival. If it were, we would have been revived by now.

Everyone who has ever been used in revival has had to break free from the world around them so they could be yoked to God and married to his purposes. We are in the world, but we must not be of the world. We are also clearly told by God that we are not to love the world (1 John 2:15-17). If we do, we find that it is pulling us away from what God is calling us toward. We therefore need to make sure we choose him and not the dictates of the world system.

Everyone has a world system, but we must remember that one day we will pass out of that world; the only thing that will matter then will be the fruit that we bear before the Lord. We must make up our minds that we are going to surrender our lives, we are going to allow ourselves to be set apart. Once we have determined that and have begun to walk that road, no matter how strong the pulls of the world are, or how corrupt it may be, we will remain set apart unto our God, Nazirites separated from others and purified to reflect the glory of God.

Prison Gate No. 3: The Works of the Devil

> *As for you, you were dead in your transgressions and sins, in which you used to live when you followed the ways of this world and of the **ruler of the kingdom of the air**, the spirit who is now at work in those who are disobedient. All of us also lived among them at one time, gratifying the cravings of our sinful nature and following its desires and thoughts. Like the rest, we were by nature objects of wrath.*
>
> Ephesians 2:1-3 (emphasis mine)

Ephesians 2:1-3 says that there are three things that hold people captive and that bring spiritual death, and that Jesus Christ came to rescue us from those things. One of these is the world system. When we live according to the ways of the world and the thinking of the world, we allow the world to dictate us, to shape us, mold us, and guide us into its patterns and ways. The Bible tells us that we are not to be like the world; we are to be like Christ. This is one gate that needs to be opened.

The second gate is the lust of the flesh, the thoughts and desires of our sinful nature. We need to begin to look at the besetting sins, how they can come in and shape us, become a part of us, and begin to make us who we think we are. Jesus Christ came so that sin would not be our master and would not control us.

The third prison gate is the works of the ruler of the kingdom of the air. This is the prison gate we are going to look at in this section.

Just as there is a hierarchy in the angelic realm, such as angels, archangels, seraphim, cherubim, etc, there is also a hierarchy of dark spiritual forces, including principalities, powers, rulers, and spiritual hosts of wickedness over territories. These spiritual powers and principalities of darkness over territories can begin to affect the whole spiritual environment over an area. For instance, in a particular area, you may find that darkness is thick over a territory and that the things of God (faith, prayer, and love, for instance) are difficult to do. You may yourself struggling in prayer. It is much harder in that area than where you come from because the spiritual powers of darkness are strong and thick over that territory.

You may go into another territory and find that it is bent toward greed or lust. You can feel the pulls of those forces in ways that you have not experienced before. In another territory, churches may be flourishing, with many people coming to faith. You realize that it is not because there is better preaching there; there is literally a spiritual environment over that territory that has pushed back the darkness and it is allowing the kingdom of God to be made manifest on the earth. You can even see this in the homes, businesses, and lifestyles of the people in the area, whether the darkness has grown stronger in the spiritual realm over that territory or whether it has been pushed back and the life and kingdom of God is allowed to flourish.

There are spiritual territories over cities and areas that are so strong that you can see that the area is affected by a spiritual power. This spiritual force can hold people captive every bit as much as the flesh and the ways of the world can. This spiritual reality I am talking about not only affects individuals and the immediate territory around us, it can spread across an entire city. You could say that it gives the area its character. People drive into a city and the moment they get there they sense the spiritual atmosphere in the city. Most cities, like Los Vegas, develop a personality, a reputation, even an image that has been affected by what spiritual forces of darkness drive that city, and the people who live there are usually living under the dictates of those spiritual forces and being affected by them far more than they have ever realized.

The Spiritual Environment in Cities. In the spiritual realm over some cities there is a strong environment of greed. Everybody works as fast as possible; they are hungry for position and prestige. Money may be the most important thing in life to them. They are ruthless operators and ruthless negotiators. They will get the maximum out of you, whether its your time, energy, money, attention, etc, without caring whether that is fair. Their primary ambition is to get the most they can for themselves.

When you step into that city, you feel the spiritual environment of greed. It will make you feel insecure deep inside and as if you feel you need to protect yourself. The speed and hecticness of the city will draw you in.

The spiritual atmosphere over other cities creates an environment where lust is very strong. If you go there, you can feel it in the air and in everything and every person around you. You will begin to see the suggestion of it in their every gesture. You will see it on the faces of the people, in their unspoken actions. Some places will have a stronger sense of it than others. Nobody will need to tell you what you are sensing; you may even feel yourself being drawn in or tempted with thoughts that are not normal to you.

Other cities convey an attitude of depression. Everybody feels low, everybody is in self-pity, everyone wants to be patted and told that they are the best. The moment you don't say the right thing they take offense. You feel the oppression all around you. You see it in the faces of the people and hear it in their expressions.

What Creates This Spiritual Environment? Where does this spiritual environment come from? If the people in a city begin to a lifestyle – a way of life – that goes against the ways of God, the whole city can begin to be built up in a way that draws demonic spiritual forces in the heavenly realms. These forces begin to drive the darkness, such as greed, lust, or pity, even more strongly. If the people in the city begin living this way, they are giving even more power to these spiritual powers and principalities in their territory, which then push the people even stronger into this ungodliness. The forces of these dark territorial principalities are pushing and affecting the thinking, lifestyle, and relationships of the people in the city.

It is not so difficult for the people in the city to be controlled by these demonic powers. Why? Because they already have the seeds of this influence inside them. The demonic power fans and excites those feelings to increase their impact and influence on the people, and then even to add more thoughts to entrench those feelings.

As people submit themselves to this manipulation, they become open to even more lies being added to their thoughts. The demonic influence on them becomes stronger. Now they begin to reason, "Things are like this. I can also do that. If people treat me like this, I might as well do this." These additions were not there in the beginning, but because they did not fight what came into their minds they became victims of this outside manipulation from dark forces.

Once this manipulation starts, we begin to have more dark thoughts and feelings, and then we begin to get hurt. When we get hurt, more lies come, which make us go deeper into self-reliance and self-protection. The way we are reacting is giving legal authority to the demonic power to control our lives. Whether we are born again or not born again, we are coming under the influence of the spirit of the air, we are being conformed to the character of the city, the same atmosphere and forces that drive the ungodly in the city.

The Spiritual Environment Over Territories. In the same way that demonic forces and influences create the spiritual environment over a city, principalities can get entrenched over territories. Principalities are a combination of spirits that control different forces over the city. They are different spirits that are all submitted to one spirit: the ruler of the kingdom of the air (Ephesians 2:2), "the spirit who is now at work in those who are disobedient."

All those people in a territory who do not know Jesus Christ simply fall victims and slaves to this power. Those of us who do know Jesus Christ but who do not pay attention to what is going on in the spiritual realm will also become victims. On one hand, we love Jesus, confess the Word of God, and pray for the change of the city; on the other hand, however, we do what the principalities and powers over the city dictate us to do. We embrace the lies and the deceptions of the rulers of the spiritual environment, and we come to love the things that the city loves.

Deep inside we are shielding the status quo of the city. This is sinful on our part because it means we have turned aside from the ways of God and been seduced by the enemy to walk in the ways of darkness. This is what God considers "wicked ways," and is what he asks us to forsake so that he can hear us when we cry out to him: "If my people, who are called by my name, will humble themselves and pray and seek my face and turn from their wicked ways, then will I hear from heaven and will forgive their sin and will heal their land" (2 Chronicles 7:14).

When we begin to fall to the dictates of the darkness over our territories, it also begins to affect the way we think. The Word says that the truth will set us free (John 8:32). Therefore, if we are not living by the Word of God, then we must be in bondage.

Once we begin to shield and help entrench the principalities over our territory, we begin to follow our own thoughts and desires – rather than God's thoughts and desires – in how to manage our lives and the institutions around us, such as how to preserve our marriages, how to raise our children, how to handle our finances, how to engage in economic activity. It affects how we look at political situations in our country, what we think of entertainment, and what we think about all the day-to-day realities in our nation.

Do you realize what is driving us and allowing us to remain in bondage to the dark spiritual environment we are living in? Our opinions and our ways of thinking. We may be Christians, we may go to church every week, but if we aren't walking in the ways of God and allowing him to have full control of our hearts and minds, we are allowing ourselves to be under the control of the principalities of darkness.

How Do We Change the Spiritual Environment? Once we come to recognize the spiritual environment around us, our only response is to turn to the Lord. We cry out, "Lord, you know my heart. I want to follow you. I want to do your will. I know that if I give you my life you will not only change me, but transform others around me. I want to give myself to attract your presence in my family, my home, my workplace, and my community. I want to draw your presence, oh my God."

If you persistently continue to pursue the Lord, the victory will eventually come. A new presence will come into your home. You will soon see your family members turning to God. You will begin to see the spiritual environment that surrounds you become brighter and brighter. We will experience the presence of God drawing near. You will begin to be set free from the influence and power of the principalities of the territory in which you live.

If our hearts are truly seeking Jesus, we will produce an environment conducive to the Holy Spirit. If our hearts are not seeking Jesus, but are after something else, we will be creating a system that is closed to the Holy Spirit.

The Spiritual Environment Over the Nation. There is a religious atmosphere that is over every nation. Revival always breaks that spiritual ceiling. What creates revival is that it provokes people to break the status quo and desire more of God. They say, "I just want Christ and only Christ." Once a few people break through and God's presence comes, others notice it and like it; God's presence attracts people to Christ.

We must break through; we must be set free from the dictates of the principalities that control the spiritual environment in our territory. We must come to a place of proclaiming, Only Christ shall have a say in my life. Let the will of God be done in my life. I want to be an agent of transforming revival. Let thy kingdom come and your will done on earth as it is in heaven."

People sometimes ask me what it means to be set apart for Christ. Simply put, being set apart means releasing myself into the hands of God and not believing that I have to be a victim to sin, to the world, or to the prince of the power of the air. As I give myself to Christ, there is victory in him, power in him, and authority in him. I do not have to submit to these things as though I am their slave. Being set apart is choosing to be free in Christ! Surrender always has a degree of sacrifice and pain, but it always results in great release and authority.

Conclusion

Even as we look at the besetting sins, the world system, and the weapons the enemy uses to try to keep us from seeking after Christ, we begin to wonder how we will ever get free of these prison gates. We need to realize that we do not get free by our own power, but by the power of Christ. As we abandon ourselves to him, he does the work in us that we cannot do.

> We do not get free by our own power, but by the power of Christ. As we abandon ourselves to him, he does the work in us that we cannot do.

We do not submit to these prison gates as if we are obligated to them; we have no obligation to the flesh or to the sinful nature (Romans 8:12). We give ourselves to Christ, knowing that he came not to bring us to perfection, but to victory; he came so we could follow him with the fullness of our heart, with the fullness of everything he intended for us, and with the fullness of everything he helped to accomplish in and through us.

NOTE: As we go on to the next chapter, I want to encourage you again to continue to allow the Lord to speak into your heart. We must see the things the Lord is revealing to us so that we can understand what is holding us back; in humility, that awareness will cause us to want to release our lives even more fully to the Lord. It will cause us to realize that we cannot overcome the struggles, sin, weaknesses, flaws, and works of the enemy in our lives by just increasing our level of effort or by trying to be more disciplined. This truly is a work that only God can do:

> *When the disciples heard this, they were greatly astonished and asked, "Who then can be saved?" Jesus looked at them and said, "With man this is impossible, but with God all things are possible.*
>
> Matthew 19:25-26

GROUP DISCUSSION QUESTIONS

General Discussion Questions (for whole group)

What is the general teaching we are seeking to grasp in this chapter?

1. What changes do we/you need to make in response to the lesson this week (in actions, mindset, etc)?
2. What is the difference between living your salvation "before men" rather than living your salvation "before God"? What compromises can living "before men" bring to the Church?
3. What do you think this statement means: "There are sins that we do not fall into, but rather walk in"? How do the sins that we walk in affect our surrendered life with God?
4. How has the world system affected the state of the Church in our nation today?
5. Who is identified as the prince of this world? How is the wisdom of the world described in James 3:15?
6. How would you define "works of the enemy" (prison gate #3)? Name a few cities where you see the prince of the power of the air having dominion over a territory.

Personal Application Questions (for breakout groups)

1. What did the Lord impress upon your heart as you read this week?
2. Are there besetting sins that you have allowed that have become part of your personality? Are you willing to allow God to strip away layers of the besetting sin that keep you in captivity? What is the first step you can take toward freedom?
3. How does conformity to the world system pull on your life? How do you break the hold the world has on you?
4. How can we pray for one another to be set free from the pulls of the world, the desires of the flesh, and the influence that darkness has over our lives?

Weekly Prayer Targets:

1. Ask the Lord to plow up your heart and reveal the things you need to deal with that hinder you from releasing your life fully to Him.
2. Pray that God will reveal any conformity to the pattern of this world in you, breaking free of the system to be set apart for Him.
3. Pray for humility before God and man and that every work not consistent with the Word of God be removed.

Chapter 11

Corrupt Wisdom

The Spirit searches all things, even the deep things of God. For who knows a person's thoughts except their own spirit within them? In the same way no one knows the thoughts of God except the Spirit of God. What we have received is not the spirit of the world, but the Spirit who is from God, so that we may understand what God has freely given us. This is what we speak, not in words taught us by human wisdom but in words taught by the Spirit, explaining spiritual realities with Spirit-taught words.

1 Corinthians 2:10-13

NOTE: As you have read through the chapters of Section 3, you may have begun to recognize in yourself many of the things that are hindrances to being totally released to the Lord. Even as the Lord has been using these chapters to plow up your heart, please do not allow yourself to become discouraged. As we complete this discussion about corrupt wisdom and then turn to Section 4, you will begin to see how God delivers us from those things that have held us captive.

Thank you, Lord!

One of the biggest stumbling blocks to a life fully given over to the Lord is our mind. We need to see breakthroughs in our minds, thinking patterns, and mindsets, as well as in our way of handling things, which is what we are going to discuss in this chapter.

> One of the biggest stumbling blocks to a life fully given over to the Lord is our mind.

The way our mind is programmed will determine what we will or will not understand; what we may or may not be able to rise up to. If we are being controlled by God's wisdom, then we are going to be able to rise up to the high calling and purpose we have been given in Christ Jesus. If our minds are controlled by human wisdom, we find ourselves constantly confounded, frustrated, blind, and uncertain, and therefore unable to fully yield our lives to Christ. For example, we might feel we need to understand everything before we choose to follow him, surrender ourselves to him, or trust him. In such situations, we aren't being led by the Holy Spirit; we are being controlled by our human reasoning and thinking.

When we talk about wisdom, we are talking about our thought process. So when we talk about God's wisdom, we are talking about God's thought process, how he looks at things, analyzes things, or sees how things should be or should go. God's thoughts are drastically different from our thoughts (Isaiah 55:8-9). We are therefore going to deal with our attitudes and ways of seeing and understanding things because this can either help or hinder us from fully following the Lord.

> What we are being set apart from is the world's thinking, the corrupt wisdom that we have developed. We want to allow God to begin to expand, cleanse, and reshape our minds.

Many times, because we try to process everything through our minds, we don't recognize that our mind is causing us to stumble. We sometimes get stuck because we are trying to process things according to our way of understanding or the way we have been brought up to see things. We are not open to letting God shape our understanding; instead, we try to package things inside our own already established mindsets.

Because of this, one of the things I would like to ask is that we allow God to open our minds to be willing to be shaped by God's wisdom and revelation, and for us to be able to discern where we may have established concepts or understandings that may be hindering what God is trying to deposit in us.

We want to allow God to reshape our mindsets. Part of what we are being set apart from is the world's thinking – the corrupt wisdom that we have developed – and we want to allow God to begin to expand, cleanse, and reshape our minds so that we can abandon ourselves more fully and follow more deeply the things of God. The reason we want to abandon ourselves radically to God is that we realize we can't break through the things we're facing in our lives, let alone our culture and our cities, unless we allow God to begin to come in and really deal with all the mindsets we have that are hindering us.

The Model of Perfection
The scripture below (Ezekiel 28:1-19) contains a prophetic utterance that was given by Ezekiel against the king of Tyre. From verse 12 onward, there is a different word of prophesy to the king of Tyre. We could easily think the same person is being addressed, but when you look deeper you realize that two different entities are the subjects of the prophetic words. One is a human being; the other is a spirit being:

> *The word of the LORD came to me: "Son of man, say to the ruler of Tyre, 'This is what the Sovereign LORD says: "'In the pride of your heart you say, "I am a god; I sit on the throne of a god in the heart of the seas." But you are a man and not a god, though you think you are as wise as a god. Are you wiser than Daniel? Is no secret hidden from you? By your wisdom and understanding you have gained wealth for yourself and amassed gold and silver in your treasuries. By your great skill in trading you have increased your wealth, and because of your wealth your heart has grown proud. "'Therefore this is what the Sovereign LORD says: "'Because you think you are wise, as wise as a god, I am going to bring foreigners against you, the most ruthless of nations; they will draw their swords against your beauty and wisdom and pierce your shining splendor. They will bring you down to the pit, and you will die a violent death in the heart of the seas. Will you then say, "I am a god," in the presence of those who kill you? You will be but a man, not a god, in the hands of those who slay you. You will die the death of the uncircumcised at the hands of foreigners. I have spoken, declares the Sovereign LORD.'"*
>
> Ezekiel 28:1-10

> *The word of the LORD came to me: "Son of man, take up a lament concerning the king of Tyre and say to him: 'This is what the Sovereign LORD says: "'You were the model of perfection, full of wisdom and perfect in beauty. You were in Eden, the garden of God; every precious stone adorned you: ruby, topaz and emerald,*

chrysolite, onyx and jasper, sapphire, turquoise and beryl. Your
settings and mountings were made of gold; on the day you were
created they were prepared. You were anointed as a guardian
cherub, for so I ordained you. You were on the holy mount of God;
you walked among the fiery stones. You were blameless in your
ways from the day you were created till wickedness was found in
you. Through your widespread trade you were filled with violence,
and you sinned. So I drove you in disgrace from the mount of
God, and I expelled you, O guardian cherub, from among the fiery
stones. Your heart became proud on account of your beauty, and
you corrupted your wisdom because of your splendor. So I threw
you to the earth; I made a spectacle of you before kings. By your
many sins and dishonest trade you have desecrated your sanctuar-
ies. So I made a fire come out from you, and it consumed you, and
I reduced you to ashes on the ground in the sight of all who were
watching. All the nations who knew you are appalled at you; you
have come to a horrible end and will be no more."'

Ezekiel 28:11-19

A human – the king of Tyre – is being addressed in the first section
of the passage (vv 1-10). He is a king who has become so exalted in
his own eyes that he refers to himself as a god. And the Lord God is
challenging him: "Will you then say, 'I am a god,' in the presence of
those who kill you? You will be but a man, not a god, in the hands of
those who slay you. You will die the death of the uncircumcised at the
hands of foreigners" (Ezekiel 28:9-10). God speaks a word directed
at a human being who is capable of dying.

The second part of this passage (vv 11-19) is addressed to a spirit
being rather than a human being; there is no way a human could
fulfill all the things stated here. God is talking to a being that was in
his presence in heaven, on the mount of the Lord, walking among
the fiery stones. He spoke of the precious stones that it was adorned
with and all its settings and mountings that were made of gold. There
is no human being who could ever measure up to this description.

God is addressing a spiritual influence that was operating behind
the human king of Tyre; the spiritual power that was influencing the
way the king was thinking and living. God at first addressed the human being, but then turns to address the spirit being. If we read this
carefully we begin to realize that God is talking to an angel who was
above all the other angels; he calls him the covering cherubim. God is
really addressing Lucifer.

The Beginning of Corrupted Wisdom

Historically, different scholars think that Lucifer was not just a glorious being; they believe he was in charge of the worship in heaven (Isaiah 14:11-15, Ezekiel 28:12-15). He was the one God placed above all the others and who orchestrated the worship in the presence of the Lord. I want us to look at some of the things that God says about this spirit being. Below are some ways the Lord defined Lucifer:

- **The model of perfection (v 12)**
  We use the word "model" to mean that, "Of all that I've made, this one is perfect. This is the one that exemplifies my best." And God, the Creator, says to Lucifer, "You were the model of perfection. Everything I've made is perfect, but you were the model of perfection."

- **Full of wisdom and perfect in beauty (v 12)**
  If wisdom is the thought process and we're talking about the wisdom of heaven, then this verse is talking about God's wisdom. God is therefore saying to this being, "You were full of wisdom; you thought about things the way I think about them. You had my wisdom and you were perfect in beauty."

- **You were in Eden, the garden of God (v 13)**
  According to Genesis 3:24, man cannot access the Garden of Eden on earth because God closed it up and placed guards in front of its gates. Therefore, this verse must not be talking about Eden on the earth; it's the Eden in heaven, the garden of the Lord.

- **Every precious stone adorned you…Your settings and mountings were made of gold; on the day that you were created they were prepared. You were anointed as a guardian cherub, for so I ordained you (vv 13-14)**
  God is saying, "I am the one who made you that way. I anointed and ordained you to be the covering cherubim. There's nothing in you that made you become that; I did it."

- **You were on the holy mount of God; you walked among the fiery stones. You were blameless in your ways from the day you were created till wickedness was found in you (vv 14-15)**
  You don't see this beauty, glory, and adornment among the other angels; this was an angel who had been adorned and endowed

above all the others. But more important, he was in the presence of the Almighty God on the holy mount.

- **Through your widespread trade you were filled with violence, and you sinned (v 16)**
  "Trade" can be defined as an occupation, especially one that requires skilled labor. The cherubim are the highest order of angels and they lead the worship in heaven. Therefore, if Lucifer was the covering cherubim, he was the worship leader; this was his trade. And God said that through his trade, through his leadership, he was filled with violence and sinned.

Who May Live on God's Holy Hill?
Psalm 15:1-5 says,

> Lord, *who may dwell in your sanctuary? Who may live on your holy hill? He whose walk is blameless and who does what is righteous, who speaks the truth from his heart and has no slander on his tongue, who does his neighbor no wrong and casts no slur on his fellowman, who despises a vile man but honors those who fear the* Lord, *who keeps his oath even when it hurts, who lends his money without usury and does not accept a bribe against the innocent.*

Look at that high moral standard and the disciplines God requires for a person to qualify to live, to dwell, in the sanctuary of the Lord. But go back to verse 1: "Who may dwell in your sanctuary? Who may live on your Holy hill?" One day it struck me that I was laboring to commit myself to the Lord, to live the best way I could according to these standards so that I may live in the holy sanctuary of the Lord, on his holy hill, and yet I read in Ezekiel 28 about another creature who was on the holy mountain of the Lord from the beginning and he rejected it. Lucifer was where I am laboring to go, where I am believing God will take me at the end of my life. He was there and he did not appreciate it! He despised it and rejected it.

My whole being was shaken. This disturbed me for several days. I am believing God to take me to the very place that Lucifer rejected so that I could dwell in the Lord's presence on his holy mountain among the fiery stones, that I might be among his angels and worship him for eternity. This being was there! He was on the holy mountain, he was among the fiery stones, he was the most glorious among all the angels. What is it that he imagined or pictured that could be better? What alternative could Lucifer have imagined for him to reject something so wonderful?

Then one day I came upon on this scripture in Isaiah 14:12-16:

> *How you have fallen from heaven, O morning star, son of the dawn! You have been cast down to the earth, you who once laid low the nations! You said in your heart, "I will ascend to heaven; I will raise my throne above the stars of God; I will sit enthroned on the mount of assembly, on the utmost heights of the sacred mountain. I will ascend above the tops of the clouds; I will make myself like the Most High." But you are brought down to the grave, to the depths of the pit. Those who see you stare at you, they ponder your fate.*

It struck me that Lucifer did not desire a different heaven, he did not picture anything different from what God had prepared. It's not that he had another vision of what heaven should be. No! All he wanted was to be in charge of that heaven. He didn't want to be under any authority; he wanted to *be* the authority! He had no other vision of heaven that was different from God's; he just didn't like the idea of God being in charge.

Verse 13 reveals Lucifer's heart: "I will ascend to heaven. I will raise my throne above the stars of God." In other words, it was his position that he hated and despised. He wanted a different position. He wanted to change the place of where his throne was; he wanted to raise it above the stars of God. He wanted to sit enthroned on the mount of the assembly, on the utmost heights of the sacred mount.

Do you hear that? Lucifer was saying, "I'm not satisfied with where I am, with my position. I don't want to look up to God. I want to go to the utmost heights, to the highest place of the mountain of the Lord. That's where I want to put my throne. I want to preside over things. I want to be in charge." He thought, "I will ascend above the tops of the clouds; I will make myself like the Most High" (v 14). Not only does he want to be above the very top of the clouds, he also wants to make himself like the most high!

Lucifer did not reject heaven; he rejected authority over himself. He rejected submission. He wanted to be in charge. This is very clearly expressed in his own words. He wanted to be like the Most High!

My next question was, "What happened? What went wrong?" Wisdom is the thought process, which means that in the beginning Lucifer's thought process was in line with God's thought process. I went back to read Ezekiel 28, which says that although Lucifer was perfect in beauty, full of wisdom, and the model of perfection, there came a time when his heart got corrupted. Verse 17 says, "Your heart became proud on account of your beauty, and you corrupted your wisdom because of your splendor." There came a moment when Lucifer stopped thinking in line with God's thoughts, when his thinking began to contradict God's thinking.

How Did Wisdom Become Corrupted?

Corrupting wisdom is turning away from the way God thinks to adopt a position that is different from what God is thinking. What caused Lucifer, who was full of God's wisdom, to suddenly change and corrupt his wisdom? I see two possible causes to explain this. The first was Lucifer's pride in his beauty and splendor; the second was Lucifer's "dishonest trade" (Ezekiel 28:18), his desire to be in control and have authority.

> Corrupting wisdom is turning away from the way God thinks to adopt a position that is different from what God is thinking.

Lucifer's beauty and splendor were gifts of God, not something that Lucifer achieved through cosmetics or his own efforts. God said that the things that gave Lucifer his splendor – the precious stones and the gold settings and mountings, his ability to lead the other angels and the worship in heaven – were put inside of Lucifer on the day he was created. This was done by God and for God, so whatever beauty Lucifer had, whatever splendor, it wasn't his; it was God's. There was a reason in God's heart for why he created Lucifer full of beauty and splendor, with giftings, skills, and abilities, even above all others. Clearly, though, something in Lucifer must have disconnected from God for him to become proud because of his beauty and his abilities.

One day I was reading Isaiah 6:1-4. The seraphim were before the throne of God. They covered their feet with one set of wings, they covered their eyes with another set, and with the third set they continued to fly above the throne of God. Then one of them said, "Holy, holy, holy is the LORD Almighty; the whole earth is full of his glory." Meditating on this I thought, the Bible says God's mercies are new every morning (Lamentations 3:23). His glory unfolds and will continue to unfold indefinitely, throughout all eternity. Even when we go to live with him for eternity, we shall never understand the wholeness of his identity! He reveals his glory and every day his glory is new, his mercies are new. The angels have been with God forever and they have never yet comprehended the fullness of who he is.

There must be moments when God unveils his glory and no angel knows how to describe that or how to express it in worship. Maybe the moment described in Isaiah 6:1-4 was one of those moments that was full of glory. The Bible says that God was sitting on his throne; his garment and smoke filled the temple. And these angels were speechless, they waved their wings and circled his throne, then one of them said, "Holy, holy, holy," and all the others said, "Yeah!" Then they began to say the same thing. It's almost like they were speechless until one broke through and said, "He is holy. He is holy. He is holy." And all of them took up after him and said, "Yeah! Holy, holy, holy."

I see a leading here; one of the angels began and the rest followed. When scholars say that Lucifer was literally in charge of the worship in heaven, he was the one leading and setting the tempo. If indeed he was, that means that whatever he started, the others followed. Whatever he did, the others would take it up.

If Lucifer had kept his eyes on the Lord, he would have just kept worshiping, honoring, and glorifying him. But Ezekiel 28:16 says, "Through your widespread trade you were filled with violence, and you sinned." But how did Lucifer become engrossed with his beauty? With his splendor? With the importance of who he was? Possibly by focusing on himself and the influence he had over the others. Suddenly he thinks, "It's what I do that sets the tempo of heaven. Look how they all follow me." Those kind of prideful thoughts lead us to begin to think how great or powerful we are. "Look, everybody's just following in my footsteps."

If this was Lucifer's thought process, then I can understand when he started to say in Isaiah 14:13-14, "I think I should be in a higher place. I think I should place my throne up there; then I could direct things better. I want to sit on the tops of the clouds; to put my throne above the stars of God. And I want to be like the Most High."

It is so easy to get caught up in the pride of our abilities and splendor. We often see this kind of thing, both in the ministry and in secular arenas. We have to remember that God gives each of us different gifts and anointings. We cannot compare the things that he has put in us with those things that he has put in another, and we must be careful that we don't start thinking that what we have, what God gave us, is better, more beautiful, more powerful, more important, than what he has given another. When we do this, we begin to think like Lucifer: "Look at him sitting over there. He doesn't have any influence over the angels. It's me who carries the day. It's me they follow, not him." I can imagine Lucifer thinking, "I have every right to lead this assembly. Everybody follows after me."

What begins to bring corruption of our wisdom is when we start to make things about ourselves. We take our eyes off the Lord and we put them on ourselves. Then we start to think thoughts like Lucifer did when his thoughts began to be corrupted. We start to look at our giftings, our annointings, and ourselves, and we want a higher place. We begin to worry about our standing, our rights, our wants, and our wishes, then our thought processes begin to be corrupted.

> What begins to bring corruption of our wisdom is when we start to make things about ourselves.

Focusing on God's Wisdom

Corrupting wisdom means departing from a position that is contrary to the thinking of God. In other words, you begin to see God's version as unacceptable or too hard or unreasonable. You begin to question God. "Why do we need to do that?" And we find our hearts struggling with the Word of God and thinking, "We can't do that in this day and time, in our culture." We find ourselves wanting to change the wisdom and the Word of God.

The Bible says the weapons of our warfare are not carnal; they are mighty through God for the pulling down of strongholds and casting down imaginations or arguments or reasonings (2 Corinthians 10:4). Scripture tells us very expressly that Lucifer corrupted his wisdom, so we can believe that there came a moment when his way of thinking and understanding departed from God's way of thinking and understanding. That is the beginning of Lucifer's falling away, and it should be a warning to us: any time our thoughts begin to question the Word of God we should see red flags because departing from God's wisdom is causing us to have corrupt wisdom.

Corrupt wisdom: Departing from a position that is contrary to the thinking of God.

Corrupt wisdom:
- Is self-centered rather than God-centered
- Destroys
- Blinds
- Deceives
- Affects our ability to trust God
- Affects our ability to live according to the Spirit
- Destroys our fruitfulness

If we find ourselves not being able to understand or accept something, in humility we need to say, "God, I don't understand, but I want to express my submission. Please give me wisdom." James said that if any man lacks wisdom, let him ask of God who will give without a grudge. But that man must ask without doubting (James 1:5-7). In other words, don't try to reason it out in your own human thinking or power. Ask in sincere submission, believing that God is going to answer and bring the wisdom because, James says, a man who doubts is like a wave of the sea blown and tossed by the wind and should not expect to receive anything from God (James 1:6-7).

These things we are sharing are foundational to a life that is given to following the Lord. We have developed teachings in the Church today that make men believe they have the liberty to question God's Word, his wisdom, and his right to say the things he says. We even say things like, "I can't accept a God who is like that." Some people even contend with Scripture, saying things like, "God, I can't receive that. I can't obey or believe that." Why do we think we have the prerogative to pick and choose with God? We have corrupted our wisdom.

The Bible clearly says that all things were made by God and for God (Colossians 1:16), which means that you are not yourself for yourself; you are yourself for God. Therefore, if you don't understand something or feel you are unable to obey something, remember that you are not here for yourself, you are here for God. Go to him who you belong to and ask, "What does this mean and how do I fit into it? How can I obey this direction that you are giving?"

Corrupt Wisdom Is Self-Centered Rather Than God-Centered

How could Lucifer have gotten to such a place of questioning God? Self-centeredness. I believe he took his eyes off the One who deserves the glory and focused on himself. The moment we see ourselves and not God, we are in danger of our wisdom being corrupted. The moment we focus on ourselves, we begin to think how great we are, how important we are, and how much our role determines what happens around us, no matter whether these thoughts are true or not. And the moment we begin to think like that we begin to think the position we are in is not exactly where we are supposed to be, and that the people around us need to pay more attention to who we are and what we are able to do.

> The moment we see ourselves and not God, we are in danger of our wisdom being corrupted.

I can relate with this. We have all experienced these thoughts and feelings. I have known them several times over the years, and there have been times when they have driven me. There are times when I look back and I feel so ashamed of myself.

The moment we stop seeing God we see ourselves. While we see ourselves, we can no longer connect with God's heart. We become like the center of gravity and everything revolves around us. We become the center of the world. We begin to think that everybody should do what they do in consideration of how we think and how we feel, how much we have done and what we desire, and we get so irritated when they don't.

Have you ever felt irritated in a service because a worship team sang a song in a version you aren't used to? Or been frustrated because someone sang a song slower than the tempo you're used to? Why? They aren't singing it the way you want them to. You forget there is One who knows everything and loves all versions. You think everything rotates around you. Who says you have to like it? Worship is not for you; it's for God. Your wisdom has been corrupted.

It's really easy to be engrossed in our own world and think everything rotates around us. We don't get irritated because God is the center of life; we get irritated because *we* aren't the center of life. We get irritated the moment we think, "They don't think about me. How could someone do that without thinking how it's going to affect me?"

They are supposed to know your thoughts and desires, your likes and dislikes. If we don't check our hearts, we all go that way. It's almost like we think, "I'm the center of the world. You can't figure out how to please me?"

Corrupt Wisdom Destroys

Lucifer's wisdom became corrupted because of his own beauty and splendor. This is also the way our wisdom becomes corrupted. You start thinking about ourselves in ways that God does not think about you. You start thinking about your strengths, your abilities, your beauty, your splendor, and then how you relate with others in a way that God does not think. In that moment your thinking has gone off track, it has been corrupted. Then corrupt wisdom begins to work, and corrupt wisdom *destroys*! It's like a black cloud that puts out the lights. The moment we begin to entertain corrupt wisdom, it switches out the lights of our lives and darkness begins to flow in.

This happens to everyone if we don't pay attention to our Maker and make him the center of our existence. The Bible says that all things were made by God and for God; not for us. We cannot make things about us (Colossians 1:16); we cannot rotate the world around us.

Have you ever been in a situation where you were right with God and your heart was at peace, then someone spoke something that you disagreed with or something happened that you disliked? The moment you let the irritation or frustration come in, you literally feel your peace going away. Your clarity fades away, and it's like the lights have been switched off. The longer you allow yourself to dwell on that, the more the darkness takes over. The more powerful your thoughts get. But if you stop and say, "No, I will not let this take my heart," you come back to that place of peace. Suddenly clarity comes back in, peace comes in, and the light comes back in.

That is because corrupt wisdom blinds; it numbs the heart. The longer we allow it to abide, the more our hearts go dead. We lose conviction, we become numb, and we cease to care. It is in times like this when we find ourselves speaking things that we would never say when we are at rest in the Lord. We find ourselves doing things we would never do or allowing things to drift that we wouldn't allow at other times.

As long as you are under that cloud, it kills something of the life that is in you. It's like the fountains are being clogged and dried up. Corrupt wisdom has got the power to defile, numb, paralyze, and make us unable to do what we know is right. Corrupt wisdom pours in slumber; so much slumber that even when we know what we are doing is not right, there's nothing in our will left to do something about it.

I heard someone say once that when you stop caring you start dying. When you get to a place where you are saying, "Whatever" or "I don't care," death starts taking over. It starts killing things. You know that a relationship begins to die when you stop caring; this happens in our relationship with God, too.

Corrupt Wisdom Blinds

Something else struck me while I was meditating on the destructive power of corrupt wisdom. The Bible says that one third of the angels in heaven followed Lucifer (Revelation 12:4). Isaiah 28 and Ezekiel 14 show the corrupted desires in one being, which he somehow communicate with the angels. One third of the angels believed him so much that they were willing to take up arms and fight against the other angels who were standing on the side of the Lord. That is blindness beyond explanation. You are in heaven and you are going to go against the One who created you? He made you! You're suddenly going to take up arms with another creature to fight against the forces of the Creator? That is blindness beyond my understanding.

This is total corruption. Something must have died inside of Lucifer. Truthfully, that's what alarms me. There is something that is destructive to the point of death in corrupt wisdom. It kills and – if allowed – it kills completely. These angels were completely lost. The Bible says that they were defeated and banished from the presence of God, never to be restored again (Ezekiel 28:16,19).

And what it alerts in my mind is, "Oh, God, the most important thing I should be doing is staying in line with your wisdom by not allowing my heart to open up to corrupt wisdom." The Bible says in 1 Corinthians 1:30 that Christ Jesus has become our wisdom, and the Holy Spirit ministers that wisdom to us (Isaiah 11:2).

Corrupt Wisdom Deceives

Genesis 1:28 has got a very interesting command from the Lord:

"God blessed them and said to them, 'Be fruitful and increase in number; fill the earth and subdue it. Rule over the fish of the sea and the birds of the air and over every living creature that moves on the ground.'" The word "subdue" is a military term and means a forceful way of putting things where they belong, or quelling rebellion, or forcing people to submit. Before Adam had sinned and nothing had gone wrong yet, while everything was still in its right order, God told Adam to *subdue*.

What is it that Adam is going to subdue? The all-knowing God knows there is a force that has been thrown from heaven to earth. He knows it is going to try to pull things out of his order and that it's going to try to talk Adam out of following God's way and his wisdom. God is preparing Adam and giving him the command to subdue and have dominion.

Unfortunately, the very first time we see it happening, man falls for it. The serpent is deceitful: "Did God say you cannot eat of all the trees of the garden?" "No," says Eve, "He said we could eat of all but the tree in the middle of the garden. The day we shall eat or touch it we shall surely die." The serpent responded, "You will surely not die. God said that? Let me tell you, God knows that the day you eat of it you will be like him, knowing good and evil."

Wisdom is about the thought process of God, the way God thinks. At first, Eve was in agreement with the wisdom of God, who told them not to eat, because if they ate they would die. Another version of wisdom – corrupted wisdom – told her, "You will not die! He said that? He just doesn't want you to be like him. He knows that the day you eat you shall be like him. You will have wisdom like his." And "When the woman saw that the fruit of the tree was good for food and pleasing to the eye, and desirable for gaining wisdom, she took some and ate it" (Genesis 3:6). Which wisdom was she gaining? The corrupted wisdom that has been marketed to her, the wisdom that would make her be like God, knowing good and evil.

Do you see that the same root that was in heaven is being presented to man in the Garden of Eden and man falls for it? It corrupts them. Why did Jesus die? Because it was impossible to restore us after that corruption. He couldn't come back to the position of the original plan of God. It corrupts completely. It necessitated the Son of God to come, die, pay the price, and give us a completely new start.

Corrupt Wisdom Affects Our Ability to Trust God

God's wisdom tells us that we are in the world but not of the world (John 15:19). Paul says, "I did not come preaching worldly wisdom; I speak another type of wisdom" (1 Corinthians 2:13)This is the wisdom from above. It is not understood by the natural mind, but only by the discerning of the Spirit. The Spirit of God discerns the heart of God, just as the spirit of man discerns the heart of man. Natural man cannot even understand these things, they are foolishness to him, but spiritual man is able because we have the mind of Christ (1 Corinthians 2:14-16). And who is Christ? Christ is the Word of God, the will of God, the heart of God, the wisdom of God. He is the one that came from the Lord.

Man fell in the Garden of Eden because of corrupt wisdom. Eating the fruit didn't change Eve; her thoughts changed before she even touched the fruit. As she was speaking to the serpent what she believed changed and she began to see that the fruit was good for food. Something changed about her attitude to the fruit. Before, she had agreed with God that it was poison, but afterward she thought that it was good for food and desirable to bring wisdom. Whose wisdom?

God intended that man should live from every Word that came from his mouth (Matthew 4:4), which is his wisdom. But now, because of the deceitful corrupt wisdom of the serpent, man began to desire another type of wisdom. That is what destroyed mankind from the beginning, and it is still what brings destruction to us today.

Mankind has been affected by corrupted wisdom since the fall of Adam. Only a few generations after Cain killed Abel, the Bible says that, "the LORD saw how great man's wickedness on the earth had become, and that *every inclination of the thoughts of his heart was only evil all the time*" (Genesis 6:5; emphasis mine). Immediately after the flood, as Noah sacrificed burnt offerings to the Lord, we read, "The LORD smelled the pleasing aroma and said in his heart: 'Never again will I curse the ground because of man, even though *every inclination of his heart is evil from childhood*" (Genesis 8:21; emphasis mine). From the day the serpent convinced Eve to question God's wisdom, the inclination of man's heart has been evil.

Romans 1:28 says, "Furthermore, since they did not think it worthwhile to retain the knowledge of God, he gave them over to a depraved mind, to do what ought not to be done." When we choose to depart from God's wisdom, knowledge, or way of thinking, God says,

"Fine, you shall eat the fruits of your choice." God gave man who had corrupted his wisdom over to their depraved mind to things that ought not to be done, and they became filled with all wickedness, evil, greed, and depravity; they are full of envy, murder, strife, deceit, and malice. They are gossips, slanderers, God-haters, insolent, arrogant and boastful. And they invent ways of doing evil, disobey their parents, and are senseless, faithless, and ruthless. Since they ignore God's righteous decree, those who do such things deserve death (Romans 1:28-32, 6:23).

Humans not only continue to do these very things, they also approve of others who do them. That is definitely thinking in a way that is contrary to God's wisdom. They know that those who do such things deserve death, but they not only continue to do them, they encourage others who do them, making it acceptable and okay.

What are we dealing with right now in history? We have full access to God's council, but are living in a generation that has turned away from his Word and said, "We will not follow that. We will create our own code. It's okay to live like this, to do that. It's okay." They tell each other, "Don't worry. The God we serve is so good he cannot hold up that word forever, so you go ahead and do that." They say, "Peace, peace," when there is no peace and call good evil and evil good (Isaiah 5:20).

Corrupt Wisdom Affects Our Ability to Live According to the Spirit

Our attitude determines our fruitfulness and our ability to fulfill God's heart desire. One of the greatest obstacles that we have embedded within the Church today (and I am part of the Church and so struggle with this, too) is a wrong attitude toward God's Word and toward the requirements of God; this is corrupt wisdom. The Bible says to put off the old man and put on the new man, who is the righteousness of God (Ephesians 4:22-24). Romans 12:2 says, "Do not conform any longer to the pattern of this world, but be transformed by the renewing of your mind."

> Our attitude determines our fruitfulness and our ability to fulfill God's heart desire.

In 1 Corinthians 2:10-16, Paul tells the Corinthians that their thinking is like human, natural thinking, which fell in Eden and was corrupted and rejected by God. Their thinking needed to be redeemed, and then Christ would become their wisdom. He was telling them that the way they think is worldly and of mere man. But he also gave them the hope that we can have the mind of Christ.

Our sinful nature is the carnal nature, the flesh, the old man, the human nature, from which God says we must be saved (see Romans 8:1-8). Through Christ, we can be saved from the old nature and into the new nature, that nature that we adopted that was in the likeness of God.

> *Therefore, there is now no condemnation for those who are in Christ Jesus, because through Christ Jesus the law of the Spirit of life set me free from the law of sin and death. For what the law was powerless to do in that it was weakened by the sinful nature, God did by sending his own Son in the likeness of sinful man to be a sin offering. And so he condemned sin in sinful man, in order that the righteous requirements of the law might be fully met in us, who do not live according to the sinful nature but according to the Spirit. Those who live according to the sinful nature have their minds set on what that nature desires; but those who live in accordance with the Spirit have their minds set on what the Spirit desires. The mind of sinful man is death, but the mind controlled by the Spirit is life and peace; the sinful mind is hostile to God. It does not submit to God's law, nor can it do so. Those controlled by the sinful nature cannot please God.*
>
> Romans 8:1-8

How do we know whether we are living according to the flesh or according to the Spirit? Romans 8:5 says that, "Those who live according to the sinful nature have their minds set on what that nature desires." If our minds are trying to accomplish or fulfill the desires of our carnal nature, then we should accept that we are carnal and determine to do something about it. If we call ourselves spiritual and yet fulfill the desires of the sinful nature, Galatians 5:21 says, "those who live like this will not inherit the kingdom of God."

> *So I say, live by the Spirit, and you will not gratify the desires of the sinful nature. For the sinful nature desires what is contrary to the Spirit, and the Spirit what is contrary to the sinful nature. They are in conflict with each other, so that you do not do what you want. But if you are led by the Spirit, you are not under law. The acts of*

the sinful nature are obvious: sexual immorality, impurity and de-
bauchery; idolatry and witchcraft; hatred, discord, jealousy, fits of
rage, selfish ambition, dissensions, factions and envy; drunkenness,
orgies, and the like. I warn you, as I did before, that those who live
like this will not inherit the kingdom of God. But the fruit of the
Spirit is love, joy, peace, patience, kindness, goodness, faithfulness,
gentleness and self-control. Against such things there is no law.
Those who belong to Christ Jesus have crucified the sinful nature
with its passions and desires. Since we live by the Spirit, let us keep
in step with the Spirit.

Galatians 5:16-25

Praise God for the truth that if we follow the Spirit, we will not fulfill the desires of the flesh, that we have crucified the sinful nature, along with its passions and desires!

Because the works of the flesh are manifest, even if you appear or sound spiritual, the fruit of what is going on in your heart will show themselves, as seen in the Scripture above. The Word says that wisdom that makes us do these things is not from God, it is of the world, of the flesh, and of Satan (1 John 2:16), "but those who live in accordance with the Spirit have their minds set on what the Spirit desires" (Romans 8:5).

Do you hear the standard being set? How do we know we are living according to the flesh or to the Spirit? Examine our mind and the fruit in our life. Those who live according to the flesh have their minds set on what the flesh desires and treasures; those who live according to the Spirit have their minds set on what the Spirit desires and promotes.

Romans 8:6-8 makes this statement a bit clearer: "For to be carnally minded is death, but to be spiritually minded is life and peace. Because the carnal mind is enmity against God; for it is not subject to the law of God, nor indeed can be. So then, those who are in the flesh cannot please God" (NKJV). To be carnally minded leads to death and those who live in the carnal mind – who are controlled by the carnal mind – are enemies of God; it is impossible for them to even submit. This is a serious matter, and it is crucial that we settle whether we are being controlled by the carnal nature or by the Spirit.

Our minds are strong indicators of the nature that we are in – are we following the flesh, the carnal nature, or are we following the

Spirit? Examining our minds and the fruit that is manifest can show us exactly where we stand and help us decide how are we going to proceed in seeking God.

Corrupt Wisdom Destroys Our Fruitfulness

Please note that I'm not talking about indulging in sin; I'm talking about what nature we are being controlled by. Are we living in our human nature, looking at things and thinking about things according to our human reasoning, or are we submitting, dying to the flesh, so that we can live according to the wisdom of God? Brothers and sisters, this discussion is not about living in sin or deliberately doing sinful things. No. We're discussing whether we are stuck in human reasoning or in human ways of looking at things. Are you constantly putting to death your human thinking so that you can live according to God's ways, thoughts, and desires? What kind of mind are you living with? What kind of wisdom are you following? Are you living according to the desires of the flesh or according to the desires of the Spirit? Remember that Lucifer was perfect in wisdom, and then he corrupted it.

Sadly, today we are failing in our fruitfulness to God. We are failing in making an impact in our cities and nations, mostly because we are allowing ourselves to be lead by a lot of human concepts, human understanding, human reasoning, and human explanations, which simply make us incapable of rising to what God requires of us. As long as we are stuck in this place, with this human thinking, we will be in harmony with many people, but we will not be in harmony with the Lord.

> As long as we are stuck in this place, with this human thinking, we will be in harmony with many people, but we will not be in harmony with the Lord.

We talk about the lateness of the hour, but we aren't able to rise up and do anything that shows we really understand what that means. We say that the Day of the Lord is coming, darkness is increasing, and we look at all the unbelievers around us and feel burdened for them. We don't do much about them; we pass them and think, "It's okay. Somebody else will reach them." We are more concerned for our dignity and how we appear before them than about trying to pluck them out of the danger of eternal fire so that they may stand before God approved. This is the affects of corrupt wisdom; this is the affect of the slumber that corrupt wisdom pours in over us.

As the Lord reveals these things to us, we realize that something has got to break, something has got to give if we are going to think like Christ and like Paul, who said, "Woe unto me if I don't preach the gospel!" (1 Corinthians 9:16) If we are going to have those long nights of crying and travailing and saying, "God break through! Break through! Have mercy and bring your salvation!" We don't have them so often because we have so much human thinking. It's one thing for which we really need to cry out to God: "Set me free! Help me to put off the old man. Help me to be transformed by the renewing of my mind. Teach me the things that will renew my mind. Teach me how to break beyond human reasoning so I may come to the place where your wisdom becomes my wisdom."

Brothers and sisters, I have to confess that my heart desires to serve God faithfully, but every now and then I have to say, "God, protect me from being numbed. Protect me from the layers that are trying to cover my heart and numb me to the reality that we are facing today." There are times when I go for days not feeling any burden for the lost, not feeling any burden to really press through in prayer. It takes me that long to realize that something is covering my heart. I have to pray, "God, set me free. Strip away, strip away, and let me be bare. Let me feel the pain you have in your heart. Let me feel the urgency, the cry; let that be my driving force."

People may think you're crazy, but what does that matter? They don't have Heaven; they have no reward for you. Tomorrow they pass away like the flower that is today and tomorrow is no more (1 Peter 1:24). Let's do the will of the One who lives forever and who is able to reward us (1 John 2:17). Let us pray that God will awaken our hearts and cause us to desperately yearn for a connection with his heart that will begin to strip away our human reasoning and our human way of seeing things, that will show us how we numb ourselves with so many different things, and how we know the truth but we aren't living according to the truth. Let us cry out to God for mercy: "Lord, I don't even know how to deal with this, but you are able to do exceedingly, abundantly above anything I can ask or imagine."

The Word of God Overcomes Corrupt Wisdom
A few years ago, the Lord began to provoke me. He revealed that my mind is going to be saturated in something: it's either going so be saturated in the thinking of men (corrupt wisdom) or in the thinking of God (divine wisdom). I am going to be influenced and impacted

by the precepts and concepts of man or by those of God. As I sought deeper truth about this, God began to challenge me to saturate my mind in his Word.

The things we are exposed to every day – the news reports, television shows, radio programs, movies, books, magazines, newspapers, and internet – all of these are shaping our mind and the ways that we think, not the wisdom of God or the truth of God. Our minds are being saturated in human wisdom, in the wisdom of our cultures and our world systems. We need to make a change here. We need to seek God for how to begin to spend time daily in his Word and in his presence.

If we are going to be set apart to God, instead of our minds being shaped by the world, they must be shaped by the Word of God, which is "living and active. Sharper than any double-edged sword, it penetrates even to dividing soul and spirit, joints and marrow; it judges the thoughts and attitude of the heart" (Hebrews 4:12). The Word of God shows us the difference between the flesh and the Spirit, the difference between the kingdom of light and the kingdom of darkness (Galatians 5:16-18). It reveals God's heart and his desires, what he likes and what he dislikes. It washes and renews, cleanses and refreshes. It leads to light and truth, which will give us direction and set us free (Psalm 109:105, Psalm 51:7). The Word gives us the wisdom, strength, and ability to throw off the constraints and lies of the enemy and to stand on the truth and foundation of the Lord, to reject corrupt wisdom and walk in the wisdom of God (Hebrews 4:12).

When we saturate ourselves in God's Word and let it wash over us, *it* begins to shape our minds, *it* begins to deepen our faith, *it* begins to show us the difference between the thinking of God and the thinking of man, *it* shows us where we are being conformed by the ways of man instead of by the ways of God, and *it* begins to wash away the thinking of man that is corrupting our walk, our relationship with God, and our desire and ability to surrender ourselves fully to him.

It is only by exposing our minds to the Word of God day after day, month after month, year after year that we find ourselves beginning to distinguish between the thinking of God and the thinking of man. When we give ourselves to saturating in the Word of God, we find that we are being raised up and becoming more mature in the faith. We come to know God more intimately and our love for him grows deeper.

This is a part of the walk of being set apart. We have gone far too long letting our thinking be saturated in the world. Let us cry out to the One who can save us, who can renew our minds to truth, who can set us free from our human thinking, who can set us free from the craftiness of the enemy, and who bring us into that glorious light of truth.

> *"Thank you, Lord, for your wisdom. Thank you for the grace to see and understand your truth, and for your desire to set us free from our corrupt wisdom and carnal nature. Bless you, Lord. May the fruit that we bear for you be holy and abundant, and may it bring glory to your name."*

GROUP DISCUSSION QUESTIONS

General Discussion Questions (for whole group)

1. What is the general teaching we are seeking to grasp in this chapter?
2. What changes do we/you need to make in response to the lesson this week (in actions, mindset, etc)?
3. What is identified as the biggest stumbling block to a life fully given over to the Lord?
4. What is the definition of corrupt wisdom?
5. What two things may have caused Lucifer to turn from his gifts and from God? What was his focus?
6. Do you believe in the right to question God's wisdom? Do you see the church questioning what it finds acceptable and what it doesn't? Explain.
7. What attitude should you take when you don't understand God's ways?
8. How do you know if you are living according to the flesh or according to the Spirit?
9. Why do you think the Church is not impacting cities and nations? What are some of the effects of corrupt wisdom that we are facing today?

Personal Application Questions (for breakout groups)

1. What did the Lord impress upon your heart as you read this week?
2. As you read this week, did you recognize in yourself ways that you question God's wisdom? Explain. How did you respond to

this revelation about yourself?
3. Why do you think you might not be having an impact in your home, church, or workplace? What are some ways that corrupt wisdom has affected you?
4. How can we pray for one another as we seek to live by only God's wisdom and ways?

Weekly Prayer Targets:
1. Pray that you allow God to open your mind with willingness to be shaped by his wisdom and revelation.
2. Pray for discernment concerning already established concepts and understandings hindering you from what God desires in your life.
3. Pray to be filled with the fruit of righteousness that comes through Jesus Christ.

Section 4

How Do We Go Forward?

Chapter 12

The Starting Point: Surrender

Humble yourselves, therefore, under God's mighty hand, that he
may lift you up in due time. Cast all your anxiety on him because
he cares for you.

1 Peter 5:6-7

As we have been looking at what it means to be set apart unto God,
we have looked at the state of our world, the state of the slumber in
the church, and the wake-up call that God is sending out. Many times
as we look at the call to be set apart, the call to radically abandon
our lives to God, our hearts begin to resonate with the idea that this
is the call of the hour for the Church. However, we are also beginning to recognize that our hearts are not in full position to be able
to walk out this call because of the compromises in our lives and the
idols that are still in our hearts. We look at the obstacles that have
kept our hearts from being completely his, the ways the enemy has
entrapped us, or the way we've walked in our own wisdom, thinking,
or strength and we can become very discouraged.

I have been in this place. There was a point in my life when I became
so discouraged and angry with the enemy and his attacks against me
that at times I would just want to hide away in some obscure place
for a long time. I was ashamed of the way that I had lived my life
based more on the words of Christianity than on the reality of Christianity. And I had arrived at a point where I was coming to the end of
myself. In hindsight, that was a good place that the Lord wanted to
bring me to; a place where I would want to give all of myself to him.

Then the Lord gave me these verses:

> *Yet hear me now, O Jacob my servant, and Israel whom I have cho-*
> *sen. Thus says the LORD who made you and formed you from the*
> *womb, who will help you: "Fear not, O Jacob my servant; and you,*
> *Jeshurun, whom I have chosen. For I will pour water on him who is*
> *thirsty, and floods on the dry ground; I will pour my Spirit on your*
> *descendants, and my blessing on your offspring."*

Isaiah 44:1-3

But thus says the LORD: "Even the captives of the mighty shall be taken away, And the prey of the terrible be delivered; For I will contend with him who contends with you, And I will save your children."

Isaiah 49:25

When I read these words, God used them to encourage me that no matter how many limitations he had revealed were inside of me and no matter all the weaknesses he was beginning to expose in my life, he was going to lead me through them. He would overcome those obstacles. He began to build courage in my heart that the limitations, the weaknesses – everything he was revealing to me – were not too difficult for him to deal with, and that as I gave my life to him he would begin to do in me what I was not able to do all the years before when I was trying to take care of myself. I was therefore encouraged to pursue the journey no matter what the cost, and the Lord instructed me to share the same principle with his people wherever I go.

Beloved, as you have gone through this book, you may have become conscious of more messes in your life than you were aware of before: the hindrances to your walk with God, how disobedient you have been, and that on your own you cannot possibly cut yourself loose from all the numerous chains binding you. You may feel humbled by all of what you see or even a bit frustrated with yourself, but God is saying to you, "Give me your life and I will fully redeem it. I will bring it to the fullness of what I intended for you. You were never meant to solve these problems, fix these limitations, or overcome these in your own power. I am your Savior. I will redeem you and bring you to the fullness of what I created you for. I am for you, not against you. You do not have to hide your weaknesses from me; bring them to me. You can surrender all of yourself to me. You do not get yourself fixed up and then surrender your life; you surrender your life as it is right now. I am the One who will begin to do in you what you have not been able to do in your own life."

Do Not Miss God

The message in this book is not another teaching for you to store in your vault of spiritual information. You are going to have to act on what God is saying one way or another.

I am aware that for some readers it is not the first time you will have received this message to be set apart. God has already been speaking to you in various ways and at different times. Some of you may even feel in your hearts that time is running out for you. You know that you either have to obey God or face the consequences. Other readers are receiving this message for the very first time and you are taking everything in. You are hungry. You have been asking questions and now you are saying, "Maybe this is the answer." You are eager to get started on the journey. Then there are others who are saying, "God has given that fellow John a nice message, but I am not ready right now to take up something this serious."

Whichever category you may fall in, I plead with you in the name of the Lord not to miss the timing of God. Moving in the Lord's timing is a major key to success. When we are operating in the timing of the Lord, things may be hard but the grace will be there. Do not miss what God is saying at this hour.

The Journey Begins With Surrender

Beloved, how do we begin this journey of being set apart unto God? I want to share this as practically as I can. The journey begins with surrender. In this section, we are going to look at what it really means to surrender and entrust our life to God. Surrender is the releasing of our lives to God. It is beginning to be aware that I don't have control, I don't know the way, and I can't overcome the flesh, the world, or the enemy in my own strength.

Just like the law was given to us to show us that we can't do it and that we need a Savior, so are all these besetting sins, idols, bondages, etc, meant to show us and make us aware that we cannot overcome in human strength. They are to help us realize that although we tried for many, many years to overcome in our power, it is not enough. There is this sense of humbling ourselves and coming to the end of self. We become aware that we can't accomplish this in our own power. There comes a releasing of our lives, a release of trying to do it in our own power and a reality of giving ourselves to the Lord. We no longer want our life in our hands; we want them in his hands.

One of the greatest challenges that constantly comes against the set apart life is the lie that you should be able to overcome darkness; that you should know how to do resist sin. The lie says, "You have been a Christian for a long time, so you should be able to this," or, "You have been a pastor for so long, you should be able to accomplish that." There is a lie in our modern age that you should know how to resist sin, the pulls of the world, and the attacks of the enemy. People are looking at you as a leader. People are expecting you to have things figured out, so we can feel the expectations of people, the expectations of family, even the expectations from ourselves.

We can feel this lie, saying, "I should be able to do this! I should be able to accomplish that." So, instead of becoming more dependent, more abandoned, more surrendered, and more released unto God, we just start trying harder, working harder, and figuring more. However, when we look back at our lives we realize that we're not overcoming. Things are snagging us and catching us, and we're not breaking through. The work is not expanding or coming to the fullness of what God called it to, but God never expected you to be able to do that in human power. God never put that burden on you to accomplish it in your human effort. He called you to come and release your life to him. He called you to allow him to do in you what you could not do yourself.

We find that instead of walking in the humility, surrender, and abandonment that God called us to, we seem to put on these personas that "we know the words" or "we know how to do it." I don't even believe that we intentionally try to set ourselves up to be the ones who have all the answers or the ones who have all the strength. I believe it's just a lie of our time. It's a lie that is being sold hard to us. It's a lie of self-reliance and self-effort that tells us, "You should be able to accomplish this."

I am reminded of the words that Jesus shared in Revelation 3:17-20:

> You say, "I am rich; I have acquired wealth and do not need a thing." But you do not realize that you are wretched, pitiful, poor, blind and naked. I counsel you to buy from me gold refined in the fire, so you can become rich; and white clothes to wear, so you can cover your shameful nakedness; and salve to put on your eyes, so you can see. Those whom I love I rebuke and discipline. So be earnest, and repent. Here I am! I stand at the door and knock. If anyone hears my voice and opens the door, I will come in and eat with him, and he with me. This overcoming is not done by human power, nor is it done by human effort. Only God can accomplish such a work; that's the reason he calls us to abandon our lives to him. He knows that we cannot overcome all those forces that are in this society, or all those things we realize have captured us. Self

*cannot deliver you from self, and God is calling us to understand
that only he can do that work.*

Andrew Murray said that surrender consisted of two things: (1) letting go of control and (2) trust. I have always used this description to
help convey what surrender truly means. It is the releasing of control
and the releasing of my will, which is then brought into submission
to the Lord.

Surrender is no longer following myself; rather, it is saying, "I follow
the Lord." Surrender, the releasing of control, is focusing not on what
I want, but on what he wants. Surrender is not what I think; it's what
God thinks and says. His word becomes the standard that I hold my
life up to and live by. I fully release the control of my life to him, so I
find that I want and desire to be in daily communion with him so he
can lead me and speak into my life. Instead of managing my problems, I release them to him and seek his counsel.

The second part of what it means to surrender my life is entrusting
myself fully into the hands of God. It is trusting God to be who he says
he is, trusting him to be faithful, trusting him to be present, trusting
that his love is unfailing and perfect in every way. It is trusting God
to take care of me, to lead my life, to be the Good Shepherd, to be the
vine that supplies my life.

If we let go of our life and surrender our will completely to God but
we do not trust him, then we will be afraid all the time. We will shake
and tremble. We will pray and surrender in one moment, but as soon
as prayer is over, fear will overtake us and we will take back our surrender.

If we trust God to be almighty, powerful, strong, and faithful, but we
do not surrender our will to him, then we find that we are always
debating God, we are always arguing with him, asking him, "Why?
When? Will it work?" We will find that we lack a deep humility and
submission in our walk with him. Therefore, both surrender and
trust are vital to our walking out a life set apart unto God.

Conclusion
Instead of figuring out my future, I entrust my life completely to the
One who knows the plans he has for me (Jeremiah 29:11). This is a

deep place of releasing your life into God's hands. He is the potter and he shapes our lives (Isaiah 64:8). We can trust him to use even the trials of life to shape us into the vessels he wants us to be so that we can fulfill the work he has ordained for us. I trust him to carry me through the fires and the floods because he said he would. There can then be a releasing of my life unto him.

There must come a day as definite as the day of your conversion when your life is no longer yours; your life passes from your hands into the hands of God and you trust him with the whole of your being, with your future, your family, your finances, your business, your ministry, your heart, and your well-being. Until that day comes, you will keep running your own life, you will keep trying to manage your own course and fight your own battles.

There must come a time when you truly release yourself and know that you belong to Jesus Christ; you give yourself completely and fully to him and realize that he is your only hope. He is the only one who can lead you forward into a life that is fully given to God. Self cannot set itself apart. Only Christ can do that. So we abandon ourselves to Him to let Him do in us what we could never do ourselves.

GROUP DISCUSSION QUESTIONS

General Discussion Questions (for whole group)
1. What is the general teaching we are seeking to grasp in this chapter?
2. What changes do we/you need to make in response to the lesson this week (in actions, mindset, etc)?
3. Do you believe there is an urgency today to surrender our lives to God? Explain.
4. Matthew 16:24-25 says, "Then Jesus said to his disciples, 'If anyone would come after me, he must deny himself and take up his cross and follow me. For whoever wants to save his life will lose it, but whoever loses his life for me will find it.'" What do you think is means to "lose" your life?
5. What is the difference between surrender and trust?

Personal Application Questions (for breakout groups)
1. What did the Lord impress upon your heart as you read this week?

2. How are you struggling to fully release your life to God and step into a place of deeper trust in him?
3. "Self cannot set itself apart. Only Christ can do that." Share what this means to you and express your praise to God, who makes all things possible.
4. How can we pray for one another as we continue to seek to surrender our lives fully into the hands of our God?

Weekly Prayer Targets:

1. Ask the Lord for humility and a willingness to see all the things in your heart that keep you from fully surrendering your life to God.
2. Pray that the Lord will not allow you to miss his timing. Ask him to give you a heart willing to see all that may be holding you back from completely abandoning yourself to his ways, plans, and purposes.
3. Ask the Lord to prepare your heart to receive the revelation and understanding that you need to continue to go deeper in trust and surrender.

Chapter 13

Love Makes Surrender Possible

There is no fear in love. But perfect love drives out fear...

1 John 4:18

When I first began to discover what hindered me from surrendering my life to the Lord, my idols, weaknesses, limitations, and utter failures were so evident. I realized how much of my faith was "head knowledge" and not in the heart. As each new thing was exposed I would wonder, "How do I deal with this?" I wanted to be a vessel that was 100% yielded to the Lord, but I didn't know how to do that.

I was so hungry for another level. When I read the Bible, I saw people who struggled, but they overcame their struggle, they did not hide behind excuses. Finally, I turned to Jesus Christ, the only One who understands all our struggles. Jesus was set apart to the Lord and fully surrendered to the Father. He ever lives to make intercession for us He ever lives to walk the journey with us because he has been there. He was tempted and tried at every point, just as I was. He has overcome, so I, too, could overcome (Hebrews 2:10, 4:15-16, 7:25).

It took several months of searching and prayer before God finally said to me, "John, the answer is not in the direction you are taking. If you take each thing on your list, every idol, every fault, every weakness, and work through it, you will exhaust yourself. There is a better way. I am not calling you to personal holiness; I am calling you to me. Turn your eyes from all those things and look to me. Bring all the baggage – your idols, faults, weaknesses, and failures – to me. Only I can deal with them, and I will deal with them in my time. Meanwhile, the secret to walking the set apart life is love."

> The secret to walking the set apart life is love.

I was so surprised! It's not about strategies? I had been working with a strategy for how to be set apart and I had a list of ideas about how to achieve this journey God was calling me to take. I was working so hard to get to the place of full surrender.

I asked, "Lord, I know what the Bible says, but how does love deal with my selfish nature, with the works of the devil, and with the system of the world around me? How does love break that? How does love break the world's system? I know I have love, and I know that you love me, but it does not work for me in the way you are saying."

Then the Lord began to pour into my heart scripture after scripture:
- Love casts out fear (1 John 4:18)
- Love fulfils the entire law (Mark 12:29-31)
- Love covers a multitude of sin (1 Peter 4:8, Proverbs 10:12, 17:9)
- God is love (1 John 4:16)
- Love is from God and love is born of God and knows God (1 John 4:7-8)
- Do everything in love (1 Corinthians 16:14)
- This is the victory that overcomes the world, even our faith (1 John 5:4)
- Faith expresses itself through love (Galatians 5:6)
- The greatest of these is love (1 Corinthians 13:13)
- He that remains in love remains in God (1 John 4:16)
- By this everyone will know that you are my disciples, if you love one another (John 13:34-36)
- Remain in my love (John 15:9)

The more he went on and the more verses he gave me, I realized, "Oh God, if that is the love you are talking about, then I don't have it because the love I have does not do that for me." I realized he was not talking about a feeling of love, an emotion of love, or just the concept of love, but something far greater than I understood.

What Keeps Us From Walking in God's Love?
When we hear the message of releasing our lives to God, when we see the picture of releasing our hearts, our future, the burdens and struggles of our lives into his hands, even the very thought of that begins to bring peace into our soul. There is a certainty within us that this is the way of the Lord. This is what it means to be a Christian.

We understand that surrender is the only way we can come to the fullness of what God has for us:
- Only God will be able to break through those things that we have not been able to break through.

- Only God can lead us into the fullness of his plans and purposes.
- Only God can take us to those levels we can never take ourselves.
- Only God can bring us to the fullness of the salvation for which Jesus died.
- Only God can strip away the hindrances and build up the character in us needed to be vessels he can use for his glory.

Almost every child of God, deep within their soul, knows this is the way we must go, that we must come to full surrender to the Lord. But what is keeping us from doing that? What is it that keeps us from fully releasing our lives to God? It is fear.

If we really begin to release our lives to God, we get afraid:
- If I fully release my life to God, I may lose my job, it may affect my income, it may hurt my savings.
- If I fully release my life to God, I may lose my reputation, people may think less of me, they may see me as crazy or ignorant.
- If I fully release my life to God, people may take advantage of me or hurt me.
- If I fully release my life to God, I may fail.
- If I fully release my life to God, will he take care of me and my family?

What Can Overcome That Fear?
How many times have you gone into prayer and released something to God, then as soon as prayer is over fears start bombarding your mind so strongly that you take back the very thing you just gave him? This fear tries to consume us and keep us from living in that place of complete abandonment and trust in God.

How do we overcome fear? We remember that love casts out fear (1 John 4:18); love conquers all (1 John 5:2-5); God is love, and God's love is unfailing (1 John 4:16; 1 Corinthians 13:8); love is the only thing that is going to overcome the fear that is trying to defeat us. And we know this to be true because these are all promises of God and he cannot lie (Hebrews 6:18).

I can tell you from experience that the real root to our struggle to surrender stems from fear, but we must be willing to trust God and let him lead us past our fears. He is taking us deeper into himself, and he will take us through our fears into the place where we really trust him and are able to fully surrender our lives to him.

As we can see, love is the only thing that can help us overcome this fear, but the love I am talking about is not an emotion, a feeling, or something conditional. It is a love that is based on covenant.

Understanding the Love of God

The very foundation of our relationship with God is based on covenant, so to understand the love of God, we must have a deeper understanding of covenant. God formed covenant in human society so that we would understand and be certain of his love, which is solid and not ambiguous, like the emotions or feelings we can have. It is something that is secure and certain; a firm foundation that we can stand on.

Many of us in this modern age do not understand covenant because we live in a much more contract-oriented society. Contracts are not even close to being like covenants. In fact, we get lawyers to help us with contracts because contracts are not based on love and trust. We seek legal advice to help make sure we are protected. We act as if the other party had the contract written in such a way as to serve them rather and not us.

Contracts are based on self-interest, not on the interests of others. In contrast, covenant is based on love, which puts the interests of the other above our self. God created covenant to be used in human interaction. He did this because he was going to bind himself in a covenant relationship with humans.

Understanding our covenant with God will also help us develop the level of trust we need to fully release our lives to him. To help us with this, we will explore ancient covenants and then look at how covenant is applied to us today in the New Covenant.

GROUP DISCUSSION QUESTIONS

General Discussion Questions (for whole group)

1. What is the general teaching we are seeking to grasp in this chapter?
2. What changes do we/you need to make in response to the lesson this week (in actions, mindset, etc)?
3. What would a life completely entrusted to the Lord look like?

4. What would an individual, family, church, or community that is fully trusting in God's love look like?
5. Why is it difficult to fully release control of our lives to God?

Personal Application Questions (for breakout groups)
1. What did the Lord impress upon your heart as you read this week?
2. How does fear come against you? What is your response to fear?
3. What struggles do you have with fully releasing yourself into God's love?
4. In what area(s) of your life is the Lord asking you to go into a deeper level of trust?
5. How can we pray for one another as we seek to overcome the fears that hinder us from understanding and receiving the fullness of God's love for us.

Weekly Prayer Targets:
1. Ask the Lord to take you into a deeper place of surrender and trust, into a place where you can understand and totally abandon yourself in his love and goodness.
2. Ask the Lord to reveal any fear that keeps you from fully trusting his love.
3. Praise the Lord for his goodness. Spend time exalting and praising his name, worshiping him for his great love, grace, and mercy.

Chapter 14

Covenant Is the Foundation of Love

I will establish my covenant as an everlasting covenant between me and you and your descendants after you for the generations to come, to be your God and the God of your descendants after you.
Genesis 17:7

The foundation of Christianity is our covenant relationship with God. Out of that covenant is the basis by which we pray, worship, believe, obey, and seek after the things of God. It is only as we are walking in that covenant relationship that we find our hearts staying in a place of communion, trust, confidence, and security. The only way we can fully release our lives to God and go past the fears and pulls of the world system is to give our self in covenant relationship to God.

Covenants have been around since the beginning of time. Almost every culture on every continent has a history and some understanding of the ritual and importance of covenant. In the Bible, God made covenants and promises to almost every person we read about: Adam, Noah, Moses, Abraham, Isaac, Jacob, the nation of Israel, David, and the Church.

Since early on, there have been three reason for entering into covenant:
- To establish a love relationship,
- To end a dispute between enemies, or
- To establish a relationship in which a more powerful party offers to cover a weaker party.

Ancient Covenants
In ancient times, once two parties agreed to enter covenant, the first thing they would do would be to negotiate the terms of the covenant. The heads of the families from both parties would meet together to negotiate. The stronger the covenant, the longer the negotiations would take. If it was a small covenant, negotiations would last only a few months. If it was a greater or stronger covenant, the negotiations

could last up to 3 years.

They were binding themselves to these details so they would talk through what it would mean to be in covenant relationship with one another. How deep was the bond that they were creating between one another? What details did it involve? They wanted to ensure there was a clear understanding of the terms they were agreeing to, what they could expect from one another, and what they were going to give and receive in this permanent relationship.

A covenant could last up to eight generations. It would be binding on all the children, on their grandchildren, and on and on. Covenant was deeper than commitment; it was the binding of oneself to another. The families knew that whatever they possessed they were offering to the other family. They knew that if the other family had a need or a debt, they were now duty bound to see that need or debt taken care of. If one of the parties had a battle or

The Process of Establishing Covenant

- Negotiation of terms of the covenant
- Cutting the covenant
- Exchange of mantles
- Exchange of weapons
- Exchange of names
- The covenant meal

an enemy, in ancient times they wouldn't run home to hide or fight, they would run to their covenant partner. And the covenant partner would stand there beside them to fight that battle because they were in covenant together.

A good example comes from Africa. If one of the covenant partners needed something even as trivial as a cooking pot – perhaps to cook a special meal for a guest – the second party, even if that was the only pot they had and they were cooking in that very pot, would empty out the pot and send it to the covenant partner's house. Why? Because whatever I have is yours and whatever you have is mine. That's what covenant is: an exchange.

Covenant creates a bonding of life. Like in marriage, it helps two become one. All the first party has, all of their resources and strengths, become the second party's as well. Both parties would share everything. They would enter into a shared life saying, "I lay myself down for your benefit, for your good, and I give you all that I have. In exchange, you lay yourself down for my benefit, my good, and you do the same for me."

The Covenant Ceremony

Cutting the Covenant. When the parties involved came to an agreement about the terms of the covenant, which could take up to 3 years, the family heads and family members would set a date and time to gather together to "cut the covenant." This was a very serious ritual in which certain animals would be used. Bulls, rams, goats, and different types of birds would be cut open and all their blood spilled out on the ground. The heads of the families would stand in the middle of all that blood and begin to make promises and state covenant terms to each other. They would make solemn vows to one another: "Everything I have is yours. When you have a battle, I will be there with you in that battle. I covenant myself to you. Your enemies are my enemies. Your debts are my debts. Your family is my family. If something were to happen to you, I will take care of your children. Your life will be watched over. I will not abandon you. We are no longer two, but one."

This was sacred. Covenant was serious. And it was permanent.

One example we have in the Bible is Abram:

> After this, the word of the LORD came to Abram in a vision: "Do not be afraid, Abram. I am your shield, your very great reward." But Abram said, "O Sovereign LORD, what can you give me since I remain childless and the one who will inherit my estate is Eliezer of Damascus?" And Abram said, "You have given me no children; so a servant in my household will be my heir." Then the word of the LORD came to him: "This man will not be your heir, but a son coming from your own body will be your heir." He took him outside and said, "Look up at the heavens and count the stars—if indeed you can count them." Then he said to him, "So shall your offspring be." Abram believed the LORD, and he credited it to him as righteousness. He also said to him, "I am the LORD, who brought you out of Ur of the Chaldeans to give you this land to take possession of it." But Abram said, "O Sovereign LORD, how can I know that I will gain possession of it?" So the LORD said to him, "Bring me a heifer, a goat and a ram, each three years old, along with a dove and a young pigeon." Abram brought all these to him, cut them in two and arranged the halves opposite each other; the birds, however, he did not cut in half. Then birds of prey came down on the carcasses, but Abram drove them away. As the sun was setting, Abram fell into a deep sleep, and a thick and dreadful darkness came over him. Then the LORD said to him, "Know for certain that your

descendants will be strangers in a country not their own, and they will be enslaved and mistreated four hundred years. But I will punish the nation they serve as slaves, and afterward they will come out with great possessions. You, however, will go to your fathers in peace and be buried at a good old age. In the fourth generation your descendants will come back here, for the sin of the Amorites has not yet reached its full measure." When the sun had set and darkness had fallen, a smoking firepot with a blazing torch appeared and passed between the pieces. On that day the LORD made a covenant with Abram and said, "To your descendants I give this land, from the river of Egypt to the great river, the Euphrates—the land of the Kenites, Kenizzites, Kadmonites, Hittites, Perizzites, Rephaites, Amorites, Canaanites, Girgashites and Jebusites."

Genesis 15:1-21

God called out types of animals and gave instructions to Abram about what to do with them. Abram knew these were the animals of covenant and was therefore fully aware that God, the Creator, the Almighty One, was saying he wanted to come into covenant with Abram. He knew that God was saying, "Abram, do you want to know how you can stand secure? How you will know what I am telling you is true? I will make a covenant with you; the sacred, serious, permanent bond. Go get these animals. I want to bind myself to you."

Abram knew what this meant because he lived in a society that was based on covenant. Abram knew that God was binding himself to him; that he was saying, "Your battles will be my battles. Your enemies will be my enemies. You can stand secure that we are binding ourselves together. Everything I have is yours and all that you have you are giving to me."

Covenant is a complete exchange and binding ourselves to one another. When God came down and did this with Abram, he was giving Abram a security, a certainty, of what he could stand on,so that Abram could know for sure that God was going to do what he promised. When God came down in the smoking pot, Abram fully realized that his Creator was making covenant with him. Abram could then fully release himself to God in trust and faith because of that covenant bond.

God didn't have to do that. He could have just said, "Just believe me." But instead he came down to Abram's understanding and said, "I am going to make a covenant with you." We can't imagine what Abram was feeling. He had been in human covenants. He knew how sacred, serious, and binding they were, and he could say, "God Almighty is making covenant with me! Praise the Lord!"

Exchange of Mantles. In covenant ceremonies, after cutting the covenant, the two heads of the families would exchange mantles. A mantle represented all of a person's authority. The leaders would place their mantles on one another and declare, "What I have authority over, I give to you. What you have authority over, you give to me."

Remember when Elijah came and laid his mantle on Elisha? He didn't say, "Hey, God said you're going to be the next prophet." He just came and laid his mantle on Elisha, and Elisha knew what that meant. The mantle was serious.

When the mantle was placed it was like saying, "Everything I have authority over, you now have authority over."

Exchange of Weapons. The family leaders would also exchange their belts of weapons, which represented all they had to fight with, including their personal strength and whatever they had with which to stand against their enemy. They were saying to each other, "Whatever your battles are, they are now my battles. Your enemies are now my enemies. Your wars are now my wars. Even when blood is being spilled, I will be there with you. You will not stand alone." They were saying these statements back and forth to one another, binding themselves to each other.

This reminds me of when Jonathon and David came into covenant relationship. When Saul found out that his son was in covenant relationship with David, he said, "Why didn't somebody tell me?" (1 Samuel 22:8) Why did he ask this? Because he knew that if Jonathon was in covenant with David, he was bound to David and not to him. Saul knew that Jonathan would fight on David's side and not his. Saul knew this, and then we see Jonathan do just that when David said, "Go find out if your father is against me" (1 Samuel 20). Jonathan went to find out the truth, then returned and told David so that David could be protected.

Another example is when Abram and Sarai went to Egypt. Did God fight Abram's battles in Egypt? Yes. When they were in Egypt and the

Pharaoh took Sarai, God intervened: "The LORD inflicted serious diseases on Pharaoh and his household because of Abram's wife Sarai" (Genesis 12:10-20). God was in covenant with Abram. Remember: "Your battles are my battles." You see similar things all throughout the Bible and throughout the years with Israel.

Exchange of Names. Another thing the covenant partners would exchange is names. In ancient times, a name represented everything. Your name was truly your identity and reputation, your whole sense of who you were. If someone says a name, you have many thoughts associated with that name, such as, "This is who he is. This is what he has done. This is the influence he has." When making covenant the partners would exchange their names, indicating that, "All that my name represents, I give to you; and all that your name represents, I receive."

God, who was known as the father of nations, came down and bound himself in a covenant with Abram. "Abram," God said, "Now you will be the father of nations." And what did God become? *The God of Abraham.* You see that? He took his name. "I'm the God of Abraham." God is binding himself in this covenant. "You will no longer be Abram; you will be Abraham, the father of many nations" (Genesis 17:5). God was saying, "Abraham, I'm binding myself, I'm committing myself to you. Everything I have is yours; everything you have you give to me."

The Covenant Meal. The next element in a covenant is the covenant meal. The family heads and members would begin to break bread together as families, making pledges to each other. They would begin to say, "I give myself to this, that your family will never be without." They would even speak curses: "If I do not fulfill my covenant, then may my family suffer, let our harvest be small, let our women be barren." They would say all of these kinds of terrible things that no one would want. they were saying, "We will not break this covenant."

God Is a Covenant-Keeping God
God had covenant all the way from the beginning of time. He bound himself in this covenant and he took it seriously. God said to his people all throughout the Bible, "I am covenanting myself to you. I will fight your battles. I will win your wars. I will be with you, I will not forsake you, I will reveal myself as God. Your part is that I will be

your God. Give yourself to me; you will worship no other thing. Your love will be to me, your loyalty will be to me, you will abandon yourself to me, you will trust in me, you will submit to my ways. I will be your God, and you will be my people, and I will show myself mighty among you. You will be a blessing unto the nations of the world."

All throughout Scriptures he says, "You have broken our covenant." He would say, "I will fight your battles," And any time they would look to other nations to help them in their battles, he would accuse them: "You have broken covenant. They cannot protect you; *I* can protect you." When Israel turned to other gods or other sources to meet their needs or take care of their situations, he would say, "You are committing adultery against me!" It wasn't that they just started going with the ways of the other nation, they broke covenant!

The whole basis of relationship with God is covenant. It's not just a moral code, a belief system, or a religious experience; it is God's way. God gives us this security in him over and over, saying all throughout the Bible, "I am a covenant-keeping God" (Deuteronomy 7:9, Nehemiah 9:32, Daniel 9:4)

GROUP DISCUSSION QUESTIONS

General Discussion Questions (for whole group)
1. What is the general teaching we are seeking to grasp in this chapter?
2. What changes do we/you need to make in response to the lesson this week (in actions, mindset, etc)?
3. What are the six elements of establishing covenant? Discuss the importance of each.
4. What is the difference between covenant and contract? Are we covenant-keeping people or contract-keeping people? Explain.
5. How does the concept of making covenant with God change our perception of our relationship with him? Would you prefer to make covenant or contract with God? Explain.

Personal Application Questions (for breakout groups)
1. What did the Lord impress upon your heart as you read this week?

2. How does knowing the Lord as a covenant-keeping God change your love relationship with him?
3. If you were negotiating terms with God as your covenant partner, what would you be expected to give to him? What would you expect him to give you in exchange? Is this a reality in your relationship with God? Explain.
4. How can we pray for one another as we come to understand the importance of our foundational covenant relationship with God?

Weekly Prayer Targets:

1. Ask the Lord for insight into the importance of covenant as the foundation of your love relationship with him. Ask for understanding and the ability to believe and trust all that covenant relationship entails.
2. Pray that you will be able to receive the fullness of what God is giving you, and that you will be able to give all that he is asking you to give him in return. Ask the Lord to show you what that is, then spend time making that exchange with him.

Chapter 15

The New Covenant

*Because of this oath, Jesus has become the guarantee of a better
covenant.*

Hebrews 7:22

In previous chapters, we have seen that only as we give our lives to
God can he begin to set us apart from the selfish, sinful nature, from
the world system, and from the enemy. However, we are often afraid
to truly release ourselves at that kind of level to God. The only way
we can overcome that fear by believing in the love of God.

We have been looking at how God bound himself to us through covenant love. The kind of love we are talking about – covenant love – is
not just an emotion. It is not just a concept or a feeling. This kind of
love is much deeper and more profound. It is this covenant love that
gives us the security to stand, believe, and trust. It is what gives us
the security to fully release and give ourselves to God. In this chapter,
we are going to look at the New Covenant and the love that God offers us through that covenant.

Our New Covenant With God
We live in the times of the New Covenant. God brought covenant into
human interaction so that when he formed covenant with us, we
would have a basis to understand what that covenant bond really
means. When we look at the ancient covenants that humans made,
we begin to have an understanding of what it means when God forms
a covenant with us.

When Jesus came, he spent those 3 years in ministry helping us
understand what it meant to be in a covenant relationship with the
God of heaven and earth. He was helping us understand the ways of
relating to God, what God was offering us, and what he was binding
himself to in this covenant bond. God was laying out what he was
asking us to do so we would understand what it meant to be in a
covenant love relationship with God.

Just as in the ancient covenant, Jesus was helping us see the terms of the covenant, to walk us through what it would mean to be in covenant relationship with God. He was revealing the depth of the bond that was to be created, the details that were involved, a clear understanding of the terms that were being agreed to, what God's expectations are from man, and what God was offering to give as well as expecting to receive in exchange.

One of the keys to our side of the relationship is that we believe that God is who he says he is with our whole heart and soul. One of the things you see Jesus doing is helping to build his disciples up until they come to the place where they can do that, not just intellectually, but that they are able to let it into the depths of their heart.

All throughout Jesus' ministry, as he talked to the disciples, you can see that he is negotiating with them to be in covenant relationship with him and the Father. He was seeking to build them up to the place where they would believe. He gives them instructions and promises: "You must believe in me. If you hold onto your life, you will lose it." He gives them commands: "If you love me, you will obey me (John 14:23). Everything hangs on you loving God with all of your heart, soul, mind, and strength (Mark 12:28-30). The distinctive I give you is to love one another. This is how people will know you are mine (John 13:34-35). And I promise you; I will never leave you or forsake you (Matthew 28:20). The One who is in you is greater than the one who is in the world. I am leaving, but I will send another who will never leave you. You will not be left as orphans. He will guide you into all truth (John 14:16-17). He will take what is mine and make it known to you. He will reveal all things to you (John 16:14-15). Ask anything in my name and it will be given unto you (John 14:13-14). You didn't choose me, but I chose you and appointed you to bear much fruit. This is to my Father's glory, that you bear much fruit" (John 15:16).

Jesus sought to build the faith of the disciples the entire time he walked with them. He tested their faith; he sent them out to use a few fish and bread to feed thousands. Even when he told them that he was going to raise Lazarus from the dead, he said, "I am glad that Lazarus is dead, because this is going to give you another chance to believe" (John 11:14-15). At times he sent them out to do work and they came back saying, "Why couldn't we break through this? Why couldn't we deliver that?" (Matthew 17:19-20).

All along the way, he would even show them his glory, such as when he calmed the sea in a storm and they were in amazement and awe. Jesus was working to help them understand that a key to this covenant is that you must know who he is and you must believe him with all of your heart.

Jesus was building them up and building them up. He wanted them to come to the place where they didn't just have head knowledge of what he was telling them. He wanted them to fully receive in their hearts what he was offering to them and to give themselves to him. He wanted that covenant love relationship to be exchanged where they would give their full trust and surrender to God, and they would receive the full reality of what he was offering to them. But they were still not fully grasping the reality of who he was, and he began to rebuke them on a regular basis, saying things to them such as, "How much more do you need to see? Oh, adulterous generation, when will you believe? How much longer must I be with you?" (Matthew 17:17).

The Process of
Establishing Covenant

- Negotiation of terms of the covenant
- Cutting the covenant
- Exchange of mantles
- Exchange of weapons
- Exchange of names
- The covenant meal

He was really working with their heart to get them to the place where they understood God's covenant and then, in John 16:31, Jesus comes to the place where he says, "Finally, you believe!" He later looks toward heaven and prays:

> *"Father, the time has come. Glorify your Son, that your Son may glorify you. I have brought you glory on earth by completing the work you gave me to do."*
>
> John 17:1,4

Jesus is saying he has completed the work. He hadn't died on the cross yet! He is saying, "I have negotiated the covenant and they have accepted it." Just a few verses later he says,

> *Now they know that everything you have given me comes from you. For I gave them the words you gave me and they accepted them. They knew with certainty that I came from you, and they believed that you sent me.*
>
> John 17:7-8

Jesus said, "I gave them the words, Father. And they accepted it. Now let me be taken to the cross, so you may be glorified" (John 17:5-8).

The disciples had accepted the terms of the covenant Jesus offered them. He had negotiated it and then shared with God, "I told them they must love you with all of their heart, mind, soul, and strength. I told them everything hangs on this. I told them they must love each other. This is the distinctive; this is what it means to be a disciple. I told them that they must deny themselves. They must turn away from the self-life and come follow me. I told them I am the vine. I am the resurrection and the life. I told them who I am. I told them they are your children, and if they believe they will be adopted, they will belong to you, you will be their Father. I told them all this. I laid it out and they accepted it." The disciples received the covenant that Jesus had negotiated with them (John 16:31).

Remember, covenant is an exchange. Jesus was leading them to the place where they would believe that he is who he says he is, that he is offering them what he said that he was offering them, that they would believe him so much that they would then give the wholeness of their hearts and life to him and receive the wholeness of what he was offering them. "Everything I have, I give to you. Everything you have, you give to me."

Where Was the New Covenant Cut? Remember that in the covenant ceremony, after the terms of the covenant had been negotiated and accepted, the next part of the covenant ceremony was the cutting of the covenant.

Where was the New Testament covenant cut? It was cut at Calvary. Jesus Christ voluntarily gave his life to go to the cross. He came to earth for the purpose of surrendering his life to the cutting of covenant with us. After he had negotiated with his disciples, Jesus said, "Father the time has come. Glorify your Son" (John 17:1). He knew it was time for the covenant to be cut.

Even as the Lamb of God was slain, as his blood was spilled on the ground, God was cutting covenant. In the past, animals were cut during the covenant ceremony; bulls, rams, goats, and birds. Yet, here was the perfect Lamb of God being slain. On the cross, between two sinners, through the blood of Jesus that was spilled on the ground, the Father cut covenant with us.

What Jesus did on the cross was such a profound act that even creation and the spiritual realm reacted to the cutting of this covenant:

> *From noon until three in the afternoon darkness came over all the*
> *land...And when Jesus had cried out again in a loud voice, he gave*
> *up his spirit. At that moment the curtain of the temple was torn in*
> *two from top to bottom. The earth shook, the rocks split and the*
> *tombs broke open. The bodies of many holy people who had died*
> *were raised to life. They came out of the tombs after Jesus' resur-*
> *rection and went into the holy city and appeared to many people.*
> *When the centurion and those with him who were guarding Jesus*
> *saw the earthquake and all that had happened, they were terri-*
> *fied, and exclaimed, "Surely he was the Son of God!"*
>
> Matthew 27:45,50-54

The sun disappeared. The veil ripped in two. The earth quaked. Holy people rose from the dead. All the earth reacted to God Almighty coming into covenant with humanity. This act of God cutting covenant was tangibly felt by all creation.

When we look at the ancient covenant ceremony, when the blood of animals would be spilled on the ground and people would stand in that blood to bind themselves in covenant, we realize that God came and his son spilled his blood so that we could be bound to him in covenant. It is through this cutting of the covenant, through Jesus voluntarily spilling his blood, that we can now stand in the security and certainty of a covenant love relationship with God. This is not a feeling; neither is it an emotion or merit that we are standing on. We are standing in the security and certainty of the covenant that God is offering and through which he is binding himself to us.

The greater the covenant, the greater the sacrifice needed. What greater sacrifice than the Holy Son of God? What greater sacrifice than God's own son laying down his life for us? If we ever doubt our covenant with God, we don't understand what it took for it to be cut, for the covenant to be laid before us and offered to us.

The Lamb of God was slain to cut covenant for you and me. Through that act, God was saying, "I am binding myself to you so that we may walk in covenant relationship, so that you may have something solid to trust in, to stand on and believe in." As he said to Abraham, he also says to us: "You want to know how you can know for sure? You can know for certain because I am binding myself in covenant and I don't break covenant. I am a covenant-keeping God. I have kept my covenant with Abraham, David, and Israel, and I will keep my covenant with you."

As you read through the Bible you can see that every time Israel was in sin, God would say,
"Because of the covenant I made with David, I won't do this." You see how serious God is about covenant. He never breaks covenant! And then you realize, he's bound himself in covenant with you and with me. Wow!

Exchange of Mantles. In covenant relationship, there is an exchanging process: "Everything I have, I'm giving to you, and you exchange everything you have by giving it to me." One of the significant exchanges is the exchange of mantles. Mantles represent authority. All that we have authority over, we release and give to another, and all that they have authority over, they give to us. This means that in the New Covenant, we exchange our mantle – our authority – with Jesus' mantle and his authority. So what authority does Jesus have?

Jesus has authority over the spiritual realm and the physical realm. He has authority over all aspects of life. He has all authority in heaven and earth. We know this because we read it in Scripture. Jesus has authority over the wind and the waves. He has authority over Lazarus' dead body. He has authority over every demon. He has authority over human powers. He has authority over nature, even speaking death to a fig tree and multiplying the loaves and fish to feed the 5,000. He has authority over the angelic realm in heaven. He has authority as he goes before the Father (Matthew 28:18, Ephesians 1:20-22).

Before he left the disciples, Jesus said, "All authority in heaven and earth has been given to me; now I give it to you" (Matthew 28:18). Since this is part of what we've received in the New Covenant, we can think, "Jesus has given me all the authority he has over heaven and earth." Why? It's not because you are extra bold today or had a "good" day yesterday. That is shaky ground to stand on. We stand in that authority because of covenant. Covenant is an exchange of life.

Jesus says, "I have power. I have authority. And I give it to you." Now you have this power. You have the authority to enter in and to stand boldly. You now have power and authority, not because you're a great preacher or a great evangelist. Not because you have a great understanding of Scripture or a good grasp of doctrine. Not because you fast and pray daily or give to the poor. There is no other reason that you have the power and authority of Jesus Christ accept that you have entered a covenant relationship with him.

Think about this! The One who has keys to all the wisdom and knowledge of the world, who has all authority in heaven and earth. The One who can say that no power is greater than he, that nothing is impossible for him, that no mountain is too big for him, that no sea is un-crossable for him gives you his authority. Look at the scope of his power and authority, the magnitude of his wisdom, and think about him saying, "I give all this to you." What is he saying? "I'm giving you my mantle; now you give me yours" (John 16:14-15, Matthew 16:24-25).

What is my mantle? What is the scope of my authority? We look at our lives and we see our family, we see the ministry we may have. We see our own hearts and our own lives. We also see whatever influence or platform God has given to us. God has laid all these things before us, and we surrender them to him in faith and trust in him.

Many times we look at our lives and wonder, "Why am I not walking in his authority? Why is his authority not being seen as I deal with my children, with my problems, with my circumstances?" It is because we are still trying to run our own lives. We are still trying to manage our own authority, our church, our ministry, our family, our finances. We are still trying to manage our own lives and operate in our own authority instead of exchanging with him. We haven't exchanged our mantle with Christ's. We are still trying to manage things ourselves instead of saying, "Lord, I stand upon the covenant I have with you. I accept the terms of your covenant. I give you my authority and I receive your authority."

When we make this exchange, giving our authority to Jesus and receiving his authority, we stand in that place where we have so trusted God, his covenant love, and his covenant exchange that our lives are fully released into his hands. We release our faith unto him, and as we do, we know that because of the covenant bond, we can stand there and speak with authority.

You will then stand in a place of abandonment, able to say, "My life is not my own; I have given it to you." As he leads you and directs you, out of the place of submission and surrender, and a deep place of communion, you begin to really see that exchange of operating in your weak human authority and power for operating in his divine and supernatural power and authority of Christ.

Many times I find that people are claiming what God has promised them, but they are not looking at releasing the authority of their life to God. We are just claiming his authority, but we are not exchanging ours with his. The understanding of covenant is missing. God operates by covenant, and only as we begin to give ourselves to living by covenant and standing on covenant do we begin to experience a greater fullness of what he has promised and offered to us. As we begin to yield ourselves and exchange our authority for his authority, we begin to find ourselves walking in a greater sense of the authority of Jesus Christ in every aspect of our lives.

We are crying out, saying, "God, you promised me this. You promised me authority over all of these forces." We declare and claim the promises, but we don't say, "God, I promise you that I would give my life up to you. It's not mine. I was bought with a price; my life belongs to you. I don't make decisions over my life. I gave that authority to you. I don't determine how things go for me because my life is not mine; it's yours. Everything I have authority over, I have given to you. I have exchanged it for your authority." Too many times, we are standing there claiming his promises, but we don't give him our part of the covenant, which is our faith, our trust, and our surrender. We aren't standing in covenant.

Many times, because we don't understand covenant, we treat the things that Jesus Christ offers us as if all he did was make promises and we are trying to stand on them. Our faith is not always very strong as we try to stand on these promises, and we may find that we can get knocked off of them easily. But Jesus did not just offer us promises. He offered us a covenant relationship, meaning that there is a real releasing of our lives to him, and we believe and trust him to be who he says he was.

When we understand and trust in this exchange, there is a reality of authority that we start to come into. We start taking hold of these promises. They aren't just something we try to make happen, stand on, and be determined to believe. There is a reality of authority that begins to come and grow in our lives, and so when we come to this, we realize that a lot of times we can't stand in the authority of

Christ because we won't release our own authority. There is something about seeing mine and seeing what he has offered and letting go of mine and taking hold of his. There is such a profound depth of exchange that takes place in your heart that literally, authority just begins to operate in your life, to be in you. You aren't trying to do it; it is just in you.

This is a real transaction, a real exchange. Spiritually, you begin to operate and be at a different level. But many times, people don't exchange their life or release their lives, so they are claiming the promises but not seeing the reality of the exchange. They may even begin to wonder if the promises are true. But when we realize that covenant is an exchange and we begin to stand on covenant, we release ours, take hold of his, and realize that something has profoundly changed inside of us. There is an authority that is now operating that is not our own, and it is a greater authority then we have ever known.

Exchange of Weapons. There is also an exchanging of the belt of weapons in the New Covenant. Think of the variety of weapons you use to protect yourself or to make things happen in your life. What weapons do you use? Some of us use anger; we feel threatened, then we rise up in anger to protect ourselves or get our way. Some of us use self-pity or self-defense. Some of us may use insecurity, manipulation, human reasoning, cold love. We may use money or position to influence those around us or the situation we are in.

These and many other things are weapons that many of use to protect ourselves, to try to advance what we care about, or to try to gain the things we want and desire. Whatever the case may be, there are numerous weapons we use to get through our everyday life and battles.

How effective are these weapons? We use these puny, human weapons to handle our problems, to deal with our situations, to navigate our lives, to deal with our battles, and God is saying, "I give you my weapons, now give me yours." As God told Israel, "I will fight your battles. Do not look to another nation to be your defender, your protector, your security. Look to me, the God of heaven and earth, and I will fight your battles. Your battles will be my battles." He is looking at us and saying, "Give me your battles and I will fight them because we are in covenant." When you really believe that, you don't want your weapons anymore (Luke 21:14-15, Romans 12:19).

Think about this. God says give up your weapons, your self- protection, your self-pity, fighting for your rights, going with your offense; exchange them for his weapons (Luke 6:29, Matthew 18:22). He says, "Give it up. Don't make it about you. Forgive seventy times seven. Turn the other cheek. Go the extra mile. Give yourself away. Love your enemies. Pray for those who persecute you. Give up those weapons and then I will give you my weapons. I will give you weapons that will begin to demolish things, that will open gates, that will turn things around, that will extinguish every fiery missile, and that will protect and secure. I'll give you weapons that will make your enemies your defenders. I will give you weapons that will make a way where there is no way. I have powerful weapons. Your battles will be my battles."

In Scripture, when God walked in covenant with anyone, he fought their battles. You don't even have to defend yourself; he will defend you! Paul was in jail. The jail doors burst open! Daniel was in the lions' den. The lions' mouths were clamped shut! David faced a giant that the armies of Israel trembled before, and the giant was defeated! The three young Hebrews were thrown into the fiery furnace and the glory of the Lord surrounded them. They don't even feel the fire. They don't even smell of smoke. The people picked up stones to kill Jesus. He walked through the crowd unharmed. They slandered and undermined Paul in every town where he ded ministry, but his message grew and flourished and spread across the world.

It doesn't matter what battle comes against you. When God fights your battles, it's nothing to him. Ridiculously, we fight by holding up self-pity to defend ourselves, when we could be trusting the Almighty One – who can shut the mouths of lions – to fight our battles.

We will never let down our guards, our defenses, and our weapons unless we trust him to be our covenant partner. The reason why we are trying to fight with these puny, ineffective human weapons is because we are not standing in covenant. We are not trusting our covenant with God. We are not believing that God will take care of us; that he will take care of the situations and circumstances we are facing. We let the fears the enemy throws at us provoke us to grab one of our powerless human weapons instead of trusting and relying on our covenant partner, the Lord God Almighty, and his weapons, which are filled with divine power. Instead of grabbing his weapons, we let the fear push us out of covenant position and into anxiety and nervousness, into insecurity and paralysis. We don't take his weapons and say, "I can hold these because God is my covenant partner. This is not my battle alone; this is his battle. My battles are his battles. My needs are his needs. We are in covenant together. He will fight the fight and bring the victory."

Exchange of Names. There is also an exchanging of names in the New Covenant. In ancient times, as still somewhat today, name represented everything: a person's reputation, inheritance, standing, and identity. When we enter covenant, God says, "I exchange my name with you. Give me your name and I will give you my name." Jesus came into the world as the Son of God; we were the sons of men. Jesus left the world being called the Son of Man and today we are called the sons and daughters of God.

We have been adopted. We are joint heirs with Jesus Christ. His inheritance is now our inheritance. God has taken on the role of being our Father. Everything that belonged to Jesus now belongs to us. We have been given a new identity. We have been made a new creation and been given a new status. We've been given the very indwelling presence of Christ's life. The very Spirit that raised Christ from the dead dwells within us. Paul describes this as the mystery, the greatest wonder, "Christ within us, the hope of glory" (Colossians 1:27).

We can't even grasp the wonders of this exchange! We who were nothing have become kings and priests. We have been given a new identity, have been made a new creation, and have been given a new life that has divine power. We've been given new standing. We've been made holy and righteous before the Holy God, that we may come boldly before his throne of grace, assured of his glad welcome (Ephesians 3:12, Hebrews 4:16).

Before he left this earth, Jesus said, "I give you my name. You can use my name. You may use my name in battle. You may use my name in petition. You may use my name before the Father. It has authority over demons, authority before angels, power before the Father. Ask whatever you wish in my name and it will be given to you" (John 15:16, Ephesians 1:21). He gives us this divine exchange. Everything that his name represents, everything that his name accomplishes, everything that his name can win for us, he gives to us freely.

When we look at everything that Jesus offers us, when we look at the magnitude and scope of everything he promises us, we begin to see that there is no greater exchange we could ever be offered in all of life. Jesus gave us his name, his identity, his inheritance, his standing, and his glory, and he's now saying to us, "I'm offering you this. Exchange your name, your identify, and all that you have been building for yourself with me. Give all that to me and I will give all of mine to you."

What this means is that we are releasing our lives to God. We are choosing not to live for our purposes, vainglory, or ambitions, but to live for God's purposes, mission, and call. We are no longer trying to build our earthly kingdom, but are trying to seek the advancement of God's kingdom on earth as it is in heaven. We are no longer trying to live to build our own name; we are living to see God's name glorified in our generation. We are no longer living so people recognize us, we are living so people may come to know God and to serve him and love him. There really is an exchange; we no longer live for any reason but the purposes of God.

When we live in covenant relationship with God, we are not trying to build up something for ourselves. It's not about you or me. In covenant, I joyfully give up my name, and with great humility I receive his. Whether anybody knows me or not, whether I sit in the back or the front, it doesn't matter, because I have his name and he has mine. When you really surrender your reputation, your identity, and your dreams of the future to the Lord, you no longer struggle with jealousy, competition, vainglory, or ambition. This is because things are no longer about you. You are living for his purposes, and you experience the fundamental, overwhelming wonder of his life within you. All that he is and has, he gives to you. This is the greatest exchange that we can ever imagine.

This is what covenant means. So many times we say, "Lord, I ask this in Jesus' name," but we don't really understand our covenant position, so we find ourselves doubtful, timid, and unsure. Do you know how much more powerful it is to stand in that place and ask in the name of Jesus when you have released your life to him and you have received his life? When you have had that divine exchange and there is faith and trust in what he has given, there is an untangling from all the pulls and pressures that come . When you release your life, exchange yours for his, so that you stand in that place of trusting him, there is a liberty, a faith, a security, and a knowledge that you are standing on sure ground.

As God told Abraham, "You can know for sure." By making covenant with God, you also stand in a place where you know for sure that you can ask in Jesus' name.

Covenant is real. It is a real position that we can stand in, where we can interact and commune with God, and it is powerful.

The Covenant Meal. In ancient times, the meal was shared to confirm and seal the covenant. God gave us a covenant meal as well. In the New Covenant, we come to the Lord's Table and have a meal with him. We renew and confirm our covenant with him. We renew our surrender and our exchange, and we renew our faith and trust in everything that he has promised us and given to us.

When you come to this table, Jesus says, "This is my body which is broken for you. This is the cup of my New Covenant that I poured out for you. Every time you do this, do it in remembrance of me" (1 Corinthians 11:25). This is the meal of the New Covenant.

Every time we come to the table, every time we come to take communion, we are renewing covenant. We are declaring, "My life is not my own. I give it to you. I receive your life. I receive your name, Lord. I walk in your name and not my own. What people think of me doesn't matter; my reputation is not mine anymore. You told me I would even face persecution and hardship; I release that unto you. I walk and stand in the faith of your name. Lord, I surrender my battles to you. I trust you to make a way. I trust you to bring about the good. I trust you to do in me what I cannot do because it's not my life; it's yours."

If we truly treat communion as a renewal of covenant, every time we approach the Lord's Table it has a way of keeping the freshness of the covenant before us. Paul warned us that we should not treat communion lightly (1 Corinthians 11:27-30). It is a time of renewing covenant, and God wanted us to come continually, to renew our covenant constantly, to remember what he has promised us, what he has given us, what he has provided for us, what we have given to him, and what we have released unto him. At times we see ourselves wavering, but then we come back and yield to the security of the covenant relationship.

Covenant Position

When we look at ancient covenants and the New Covenant, we realize that covenant is a place of great surrender. We are laying down all that we are, all that we have We are giving everything to God. This is a place of great trust. We are trusting all that God has bound himself to. We are standing on that, believing it, holding onto it, and letting it be the anchor to our souls.

There is a place where we begin to see what God has offered us and our hearts begin to take hold of it by faith. We have security, calm, peace, and assurance. Something builds up in us that begins to give us such a sense of trust that we feel as though we can release ourselves to God like we never have before. We release our future and ourselves into his hands, and we believe him to do what he said he would do, to be who he said he would be, and to accomplish what he said he would accomplish. In that place where we are standing – truly believing in him, fully trusting him, and fully releasing ourselves to him, we call that place covenant position. That is a place we should not experience once in a while in our lives; it is the place where we abide in him as he abides in us.

The place we call covenant position is a real place. It is a place where we come to full trust and faith in God. We trust that he is going to do what he said, that he has bound himself to us in the way he promised, and that he is offering to us everything that he has. We come to a place where we trust and believe him so much that we release ourselves fully to him. And when we release ourselves to God in that way, when we come to this place of trust and faith, we begin to experience rest in our souls, a security that we have never known, and a deep and abiding communion with God.

This covenant security and love is what makes our surrender and abandonment to a set apart life possible. It is what helps this life flow and be continually ongoing. This is the place we call covenant position.

Covenant position is something to cherish and treat as sacred. I honestly believe that the only thing that is going to break through in the nations is people standing in covenant position who allow God to do things through them that they could never do themselves. It is not going to be a great speech, a good organizational scheme, a new program, or a conference; we have plenty of those things. What is going to bring change and transformation to the nations is the authenticity of the life of God flowing through a vessel that is standing in covenant with him.

Covenant position is not a place where we strive to feel spiritual. It is a place of simply being in Christ, standing in a place where we believe him to be who he said he is and doing what he said he would do. We trust this so much that we release ourselves in great abandonment to him. In that place there is trust, rest, peace, covering, and security. It is the place where we realize, "I can abide in him. I can remain in him," as John 15:4 says. This is the place where the flow of Christ's life comes continually to us and, because the enemy wants to oppose us being in this place, we must guard, protect, and fight to keep it.

The position in your life that is the most contended for is your covenant position before God. The enemy comes against this day after day after day. He tries to do anything to make you panic, to take you into fear. He wants to make you anxious, nervous, insecure, and doubtful of God's covenant love and security, so you will pull your heart back from that bond, that communion you have with God when you stand in covenant position.

We must fight to maintain our covenant position. We are at war whether we want to be or not, and we cannot just be passive when we're at war. We can't just sit back and coast; we must guard our covenant position. If the enemy attacks us at three o'clock in the afternoon, bringing fear and doubt, we can't say, "Well, prayer time is tomorrow morning. I'll fight then." You fight when the battle is present. Because covenant position is where all life flows, the enemy is going to try to cut off that life, but we must fight the fight to keep our position.

If we are really seeking to stay in an environment of faith and trust in the covenant love and exchange of God, then staying in covenant position must be one of our primary focuses. You can't just pray into covenant when you come to the communion table. You must pray into covenant on a daily basis. You pray into being fully surrendered and in full trust. You hold up what God has given to you; the promises and gifts, the weapons and instructions. You lay down everything he's asked you to lay down. You are exchanging life; not based on a feeling, but based on the fact that God is true to his word.

Many times, we are just trying to fight the battles of the day; that is all our lives are about. But when we begin to stand in covenant position, we start to become more secure and have a firmer footing. We begin to walk in greater authority and to experience God's life flowing through us. His life is a victorious life, and as we begin to stand in covenant position, our lives begin to be about the work of God instead of just being about trying to keep going. As we become more secure in that, our faith in the indwelling life of Christ begins to rise up, enabling us to fulfill the work God has for us. We begin to believe that he can do what he said he would do, and we begin to have a greater sense of our calling and the purpose that he has assigned to us.

God works in and through a person who is committed to standing in covenant position. Those who allow the Holy Spirit to take them into deeper faith and trust will start to see God in ways they never imagined, but we must remain in covenant position. When Jesus said, "Remain in me and I promise I will remain in you. I will flow through you and you will bear much fruit" (John 15:1-11), he was saying, "Stand in covenant position. Stand in this place where your life is not yours, where you have exchanged your life for my life, and where you are trusting my life to be there and to flow freely to you and through you."

Why is covenant position so important? Because Jesus also says that if we don't remain him, in that place of radical abandonment, we can do nothing. We cannot bear the fruit in our own power and ability (John 15:5).

Conclusion
Think of the wonder of what he is giving us compared with what we are giving him. There is no other deal in the world like this one, and not one of us would turn it down. We have nothing to lose except our wretched lives, faults, failures, human nature, blindness, hurts, and hard hearts. Those are the things we exchange and give up so we can walk in the reality of Christ's authority and security.

Our battles are God's battles. We don't need our weapons because he will never leave us or forsake us. The One that is within us is greater than the one who is in the world. No man can thwart the purposes to which God has given us to walk out and fulfill. We have a certainty that we are his, that we belong to him, and we see and experience the freshness and newness of the life of Christ that is within us. We take hold of the inheritance we have been given in Jesus Christ. We begin to stand in security and knowledge of his nature, of that place of communion, trust, and faith, of that covenant love and security.

We have all touched Christ's life enough to know that it is real and tangible. We know we can abide in his life rather than just getting a glimpse of it for a few moments, so when he says, "Will you come? Will you exchange your life for mine?" we say, "Yes, Lord. We will come. We will receive what you are offering."

GROUP DISCUSSION QUESTIONS

General Discussion Questions (for whole group)
1. What is the general teaching we are seeking to grasp in this chapter?
2. What changes do we/you need to make in response to the lesson this week (in actions, mindset, etc)?
3. Discuss the six elements of establishing the New Covenant? Discuss the importance of each.
4. Why do you think the Church does not experience the power and authority of Jesus that we see in the New Testament?
5. How and why does the enemy and our flesh fight against our trusting and resting in our covenant with God?
6. How do we pray into covenant position?

Personal Application Questions (for breakout groups)
1. What did the Lord impress upon your heart as you read this week?
2. Which of your weapons would you like to give to the Lord? Which of his weapons would you like to receive in exchange? Be specific, such as, "I need to release my self-pity and receive his protection."
3. How do you struggle with trusting in God's covenant with you?
4. How can we pray for one another as we seek to understand and fully trust God's covenant relationship with us?

Weekly Prayer Targets:
1. Ask for a deeper understanding of the New Covenant than you have had previously. Go through each element of the covenant

ceremony, thanking God for what he takes from you and for what he gives you in exchange.
2. Ask the Lord to help you be able to love him with all your heart, soul, mind, and strength, as he has loved you. Ask him to help you come to love others with this same love.
3. Love makes surrender possible. Therefore, ask God to help that foundation of love take you to the place of full and abandoned surrender and trust in him.

Chapter 16

Standing in Covenant Position

I have been crucified with Christ and I no longer live, but Christ lives in me. The life I live in the body, I live by faith in the Son of God, who loved me and gave himself for me.

Galatians 2:20

We can read about covenant, be undone by the reality of what God has offered us, and yet still not know how to get into covenant position or come into the reality of total, abandoned faith and trust in the Lord. In this chapter, we will begin to discuss how to do that.

As we've seen, it is the love of God that makes surrender possible, and it is the covenant that we have with God that is the foundation of our love relationship with him. However, if we do not have full faith in the Lord, we are unable to trust in his love and in the covenant he has made with us. We will be unable to come into the covenant position we so desperately need to be able to profoundly release our lives to the Lord so he may set us apart from the sinful nature, the world's ways and mindset, and the spiritual powers of darkness and begin to establish us into his purposes.

Trusting in God's Love and Covenant Relationship

Even though we believe God loves us and know that he has made covenant with us, many of us frequently struggle to maintain our belief that these things are true. We want to come to the place of covenant, but are unable to take that step of trust. We want to surrender everything to God, but don't know what is holding us back. We don't know why we can't fully let go. I believe if we were honest with ourselves many of us would confess that we have similar struggles.

However, these struggles can be overcome. We can come into a place of trust and faith in the Lord where we can take hold of his love and his covenant, just as we have taken hold of the truth of our salvation. In fact, I will equate this discussion to the gospel of salvation.

When we gave our lives to Christ, we did it as a step of trust. We didn't wait for repentance. We didn't wait for an emotional release. We didn't wait until we had overcome our bad habits or difficult situations. We just came to the place of saying, "Today I give my life to the Lord." When we professed our faith and confessed Jesus as our Lord, we knew that our salvation had been accomplished, and that it was thoroughly and completely finished. We crossed a line in our mind. We fully understood that Christ had offered us eternal life, forgiveness, and acceptance and that we had received it.

From that moment of salvation, that moment when new believers have crossed the line, they begin to think of themselves as new creatures. Does that mean if they had a drinking problem there were no more pull towards drunkenness? No, that pull is still there, but when it comes they say, "I have been saved." They counter the old thinking with the new thinking.

New Thinking and a New Identity

The most important thing here is the new thinking and the feeling of a new identity. The old pulls of the world are still inside the person and their weaknesses are still present, but they have a new way of thinking. That thinking is the thinking of faith; it believes. And it crossed the line into a new identity: I no longer have my old nature, I'm no longer going after those old things, I have a new set of disciplines, I have a new master, I have a new meaning to life, there's a new purpose to me.

Newly born-again people don't struggle with their new thinking or their new identity. That's how they are able to stay focused on the Lord and continue to work out their salvation each day. Not because they are so strong that they overcome everything overnight. It is because their faith is so fresh that it sustains them. It's just the faith of, "I am new!" Their conviction says that, "Because I am new in Christ and given my life to him, he is going to set me free. I'm not going to keep doing those things." They don't expect themselves to be resisting forever; they believe it's going to go away and that God is going to help them overcome.

No matter how much the temptations and pressures to return to their old life keep coming, new believers are convinced that God is going to help them, that he is going to deliver them from the pulls and pressures they face. Sooner or later, it's going to stop. They are certain it will not keep happening the rest of their life.

Believing God

Brothers and sisters, you have heard the Gospel of salvation; that God has forgiven you, taken away your guilt, and given you his life. He's offered you salvation, not because you deserved it or earned it. He does not say, "First get rid of your sin, then I'll give you my life." He does not say, "Prove to me you'll not turn back and then I'll give you my life." No! He says, "Believe."

New believers don't try to figure out how they are going to overcome. They don't try to figure out a new strategy to deal with their addiction. They don't come up with a new self-effort strategy for how they will manage their anger better. They believe. And it is that belief in God, in his power, in the fullness of what he offers through Jesus Christ, that accomplishes so much in their life. It begins to change almost everything inside of them, and they step across a line. And even though they may have many things trying to pull them back, it is that belief they have in God that has the power to begin to change everything in their life.

They really believe that Jesus has forgiven them. They really believe that they don't have to live in sin anymore. There are people who may have lived in profanity their whole life, but when they come to believe in God, they can't even stand a profane word in their mouth. There may have been people who lived in deep addictions, but the power of that addiction is broken as they give their lives to Jesus Christ. This belief is a real, tangible line that they step across, where the exchange takes place.

The Doubt That Comes to Steal Our Faith and Trust

Like a new believer who steps across a line to receive salvation, we need to step across a line to experience the reality of covenant relationship with God. A new believer does not try to feel something before he experiences salvation; he just believes. And we need to believe that God has bound himself to us in this covenant love; not because we feel it, not because we've overcome, but because of what he has said in his Word. Like a new believer, begin to experience God's love and your covenant with him by faith. Begin to consider that you are a new creation. The old self, the old nature, no longer exists. Don't count yourself as carnal,

> We need to step across a line to experience the reality of covenant relationship with God.

allowing your old flesh nature to remain; otherwise, Christ has done nothing.

He is waiting for you to trust him. It's not by works that we enter into covenant with God; it is by faith. By faith consider it done. By faith believe that you have covenant position. When you ask anything, believe that you have received it and you will have it (John 14:14). The enemy tries to hinder our faith by making us look at ourselves and our failures instead of at what God is offering, but we place our eyes on Christ and choose to believe what he says is true.

The enemy tries to get us to focus on ourselves, on our circumstances, on our inabilities; however, we set our focus on Jesus Christ, not on our feelings or our thoughts. We pray into believing who he is, believing his love, believing what he accomplished at the cross. We pray into what Jesus has done. We believe that our God is a covenant-keeping God because we can see he kept covenant with Moses, with Abraham, and with David. We begin to pray into that, to turn our eyes away from ourselves, and to set our eyes firmly on who God is and what he has said.

The enemy tries to confound our faith by accusing us and distracting us from what God has promised. He is called the accuser of the brethren, so don't become stuck on his accusations. To keep you from walking in your new nature, Satan will remind you of your old nature. Don't sit there and be discouraged, saying, "Oh, I'm still like this. Why can't I give it up?!" When your old nature pulls at you, turn your eyes to God. Give him praise. Hallow his name for what he has done in the covenant, for what he has offered to you in this covenant relationship. Thank him for drawing you to himself, for giving you a new life, for giving you an innocence and the indwelling presence of his Spirit. Thank him that he can work through you, and that the fruit he bears through you will not be by your power or might, but by his Spirit.

As you praise him for all that he has done for you, thank him for the Holy Spirit, who is your helper. Thank God that he is not asking you to accomplish a work, he is not asking you to prove anything. He is asking you to receive! Believe what he has promised! And then when you believe and trust in this covenant relationship he is offering you, walk by faith. Think by faith.

In your new position, receive his salvation. Thank him, exalt him, and extol him. Let your spirit rest in him. Abide in him and let his words abide in you. Believe that you are no longer operating in your old nature; you are now a new creation. You don't have to use your power, your authority, or your reasoning; you can depend on God's. Stand in faith and believe!

The Good Fight of Faith

What is the good fight of faith? To say to the devil, "I am no longer that old creature! I don't have to do anything to fight you and your accusations. I received this life by faith and I will walk in it by faith. I will speak it by faith and I will think it by faith. I will stand by faith and belief. I am an heir to the Kingdom of God. I can do all things through him who gives me strength and ability. I am acceptable before him. I can enter the throne room with boldness, not because of what I've done but because of what Christ has done. Thank you, Jesus, that by covenant you brought me into your kingdom. I am rejecting the old man and walking in the new man. My profession of faith is that I am not going to be pulled back into my old identity; that creature is dead. I am a new creature, and I will walk by the faith of Jesus."

It's not only at the time of salvation that you become new. You may realize today that you have not been standing in the right place, that you have not been walking in the right way, but Jesus is offering you covenant relationship. He says, "You didn't understand what I did at salvation. I offered to bind myself to you in covenant relationship. You didn't understand it then, so let me offer it to you today. Now you can receive it with an even deeper understanding. Take it so we can walk together in covenant."

The Battle We Fight to Stand in Position

Brothers and sisters, when the anxieties and doubts come to push you away from fully trusting God with all your heart, don't go straight to war. Turn to the One who gives you the victory. This is a key to fighting for covenant position. Instead of fighting the doubts and fears, instead of focusing on the anxieties, we turn our eyes to God and we praise him and exalt him, and begin to come to the place where we recognize his greatness, his wonder, his love, and his faithfulness.

Begin to say, "How would I stand above this as an overcomer if it

When anxieties and doubts come to push you away from fully trusting God with all your heart, don't go straight to war. Turn to the One who gives you the victory. This is a key to fighting for covenant position.

weren't for you? I give you praise, I give you glory." Exalt him! And at the end say, "Lord, I give you glory. I take my position in you. I confess these things that would compromise me, and I believe and trust that the blood of Jesus is what takes them away. I will not be bound by them but in you and in the faith of what you speak to me. By the faith of your own heart I turn to the enemy and in the name of Jesus I rebuke those dark powers."

You cannot do this because you feel power. It's not about your feelings or about your confidence. Even Paul was with the Corinthians trembling in fear! He said, "I did not come with eloquence or superior wisdom...I came to you in weakness and fear, and with much trembling" (1 Corinthians 2:1,3).

It's not about what you can do or about what you feel. Feelings are deceptive. Today you feel good but tomorrow you don't. But God is consistent. What he has done, he has done. When he says something today, he doesn't change his mind tomorrow. God is faithful and trustworthy. What he desires today, he will desire tomorrow.

When you fail or you fall, he tells you, "Do you realize you've fallen?" When you say, "Yes Lord, I do," he encourages you to get back into position. He doesn't point his finger in accusation. He lovingly says, "Do you realize you've fallen? Do you realize you're sliding away?" When we say "yes" and plead for mercy, he replies, "Then come back! Get back into position. Let's continue working." That's him. He does not condemn us. Neither does he judge us at every fall. Doesn't the Bible say the righteous will fall (Proverbs 24:16)? How many times? But God helps me with each and every one of my failures.

Our battle is not about fighting and resisting the things that are coming against us. Don't let your prayers always start, "Oh, Lord, have mercy on me." Let them start with him. "You, Lord, deserve the glory! You are God and there is none like you. You are my savior, my redeemer, my deliverer. You are the rock of my salvation. Where would I be without you? I would have no hope because there's no power inside of me to help myself. Lord, I thank you because even when I did not know how to turn to you, you turned to me. You were holding me up; you were giving me the strength to stand. I was failing, I was hopeless, and I was condemning myself, and you came back to me and reminded me of your covenant, which you offer to me for free. I don't even understand it, Lord, but I believe and I choose to step into that place of trust. I will think new, I will talk new, and I will walk new. I will put off the old man to walk in the new man."

He will do the rest by faith, as he did when you first received your salvation. You did not work it out by thinking through each step: "How am I going to stop this and change that?" You just trusted him and walked in your freedom. In those first days the joy of salvation was great. The temptation was still coming in, but you had faith in the new walk and you did not let them trouble you; they eventually went away. The same thing – this same attitude of trust and faith – is what is required today.

Crossing the Line

Today you can cross that line. Does that mean you'll stop feeling your weaknesses? No. But you can say, "That's the old man." You can constantly put off the old man. You can be transformed by the renewing of your mind. The enemy is going to come and lie to you every minute to try to make you think you will not be changed. But you can tell him, "Look here, I will not give up this freedom. I will not give it up because it's not by my power, nor by my might. I receive it by faith and he is not a liar who is giving it to me."

Even as you lay down this book and something comes against you, tell him, "Devil, I'm not giving this up. It's a free gift and I am staying with it." The moment you finish saying that, turn to Christ and worship! Exalt his name. Focus on him and thank him for the victory in such things. Thank him that you don't have to rely on your feeble and weak human power to deal with it. Thank him that you don't have to have you own personal victory and that you don't have to feel good about it before you can trust or believe him to do it. Thank him that you don't have to emotionally feel the victory. Thank him for the trust and faith that he is building up in you.

The Faith That God Is Growing Within Us

Faith calls things that are not as though they are (Hebrews 11:1). Hebrews 11:6 says that those who seek after God must believe that he hears and that he rewards those who diligently seek him, and that without faith it is impossible to please God. Today, right now, we can enter God's presence as accepted sons and daughters according to the very covenant of God. We can come to him as children who God is pleased with because of their faith in his work. We are not condemned by him because of our human weaknesses. Rather, he is pleased with us because we have believed him. Pleased that the Word came down and they believed it. Jesus said, "Father, I have given them the Word and they have believed it. So I pray protect them with your name. They are in the world but they are not of the world" (John 17:14-17).

Brothers and sisters, I am making an altar call right now, just like an evangelist makes an altar call. Will you put your faith in Christ? Will you put faith in his finished work? Will you stop condemning yourself? Will you stop identifying with dead works? Will you cross this line and say, "On this day my life was renewed. I'm not going back. I'm stepping across; I'm ready for the new wave God is releasing. I'm not going to be pulled back because I don't have to do anything. He's inviting me to step into the place of release. He is the rock of my salvation." He does not condemn you, but says, "Come, believe it!"

Abraham believed God and it was accounted to him as righteousness (Romans 4:3). You don't have to feel good or emotionally moved; our response is by faith. God is calling, "Come, will you receive the covenant? Will you come into covenant relationship with me?"

Jesus is saying, "I give you my freedom, my eternal life, my power, my authority, my inheritance, and my place with the Father. I give it all to you. And if you walk by faith I will fulfill every one of the dreams the Lord has placed on your heart, every one of the burdens that concern you."

What is your response? "Lord, I give you praise. Break the yokes of self-exaltation, self-centeredness, and self-focus. Thank you for your free gifts and for your work in my life. Please give me deeper faith and belief in you, your love, and your covenant. Please help me believe you for every promise you have spoken and know to the depths of my being that you will cherish me and take care of me all the days of my life. Help me to be humble, to be submitted. Help me to totally and fully surrender myself into your hands and allow you to set me apart for your work. And Lord, bless you. I give you praise for the finished work."

GROUP DISCUSSION QUESTIONS

General Discussion Questions (for whole group)
1. What is the general teaching we are seeking to grasp in this chapter?
2. What changes do we/you need to make in response to the lesson this week (in actions, mindset, etc)?
3. How would you describe "standing in covenant position"? How do we stand in covenant position? What keeps us from doing that?
4. How is trusting God today to work out your surrender the same as trusting him to save you on the day of your salvation?
5. What would the army of God look like if it were filled with people standing in covenant position?

Personal Application Questions (for breakout groups)
1. What did the Lord impress upon your heart as you read this week?
2. What old ways of thinking do you need to lay down to cross over into a new place of trusting God?
3. What struggles do you have in standing in covenant position? Doubts? Fears? Unbelief? Explain.

Weekly Prayer Targets:
1. Pray that God will help you see with eyes of faith. Pray that he will help you take your eyes off of yourself and be able to see that it is only through his strength that you can walk a life set apart to him.
2. Ask the Lord to help you come to a place of trust in the deepest place in your heart that he is who he says he is, that he does what he promises to do, that he will do a work in you that only you can do, and that as you surrender your life into his hands, you will have peace and rest as he does that work. Ask him to take you to a place of trust and faith that is beyond anything you have known before.

Section 5

Epilogue

Chapter 17

God Is Raising Up an Army

The Lord thunders at the head of his army; his forces are beyond number, and mighty are those who obey his command. The day of the Lord is great; it is dreadful. Who can endure it?

Joel 2:11

The power of wickedness and sin is becoming overwhelming in the many different ways – on individuals, families, governments, economies, and nations. They will be evil days, and many people will turn away from the faith, listening instead to lying doctrines. When the Day comes, they will not survive (Matthew 24:7-12).

This is the situation of our present day. It has been thousands of years since God spoke to Abraham, raising up the "set apart" nation through which the nations would come to know God. Our Redeemer, Jesus Christ, came into the world to bring salvation and redemption, and the Church was given the Holy Spirit and the Great Commission to "go and disciple the nations" (Matthew 28:19). God has given the Church time – over 2,000 years – to go to the nations and fulfill this Commission. But now the Day is near, so close, and his judgments are beginning to come on the earth. Wickedness and darkness are suffocating the earth. Children no longer know the difference between right and wrong because the line has been blurred. Churches are falling into deception and slumber. Where will our hope come from?

The Day of the Lord Is Drawing Near

Is the Church of today any different from Israel before the coming of Jesus? What is different? They read the Scriptures, they followed the Law, but their hearts had no power to overcome, just as we see in most of the Church today.

The Day of the Lord is coming near. Is the Church ready? Is the Church prepared to stand against the tide of darkness, helping to pull lost souls out of eternal judgment?

We are not living in the power of God. We are not living sold-out, surrendered lives that could turn cities and whole nations upside down. A large part of the Church is not where God wants it to be.

The nations are groaning because wickedness is coming to fullness. People are groaning under the burden of sin and wickedness and the way it is being manifest in cities and nations. God hears the cry of the nations, of the people, but his church and his people are not where they are supposed to be. They are not living the victorious, powerful life they are supposed to be living, and are therefore powerless in the face of sin, the world system, and the works of the devil.

The cities and nations we are living in are exactly like those that God rejected in times past, but he had mercy and sent us a Savior. The hour is late and the coming of the Lord is near. The time is urgent.

We act like surrender is tortuous and impossible, and the Church has lost understanding and revelation. Without vision the people perish, without revelation the people cast off restraint (Proverbs 29:18). What is God's intention in this hour? What is burning in God's heart? When God looks at the world today and sees the state of the Church and the nations, and that the Day of the Lord is at hand, what is the desire of his heart? What does he purpose to do in these dark times?

God Is Raising Up an Army

Blow the trumpet in Zion; sound the alarm on my holy hill. Let all who live in the land tremble, for the day of the LORD is coming. It is close at hand— a day of darkness and gloom, a day of clouds and blackness. Like dawn spreading across the mountains a large and mighty army comes, such as never was of old nor ever will be in ages to come. Before them fire devours, behind them a flame blazes. Before them the land is like the garden of Eden, behind them, a desert waste— nothing escapes them. They have the appearance of horses; they gallop along like cavalry. With a noise like that of chariots they leap over the mountaintops, like a crackling fire consuming stubble, like a mighty army drawn up for battle. At the sight of them, nations are in anguish; every face turns pale. They charge like warriors; they scale walls like soldiers. They all march in line, not swerving from their course. They do not jostle each other; each marches straight ahead. They plunge through defenses without breaking ranks. They rush upon the city; they run along the wall. They climb into the houses; like thieves they enter through the windows. Before them the earth shakes, the sky trembles, the sun and moon are darkened, and the stars no longer shine. The LORD thunders at the head of his army; his forces are beyond number, and mighty are those who obey his command. The day of the LORD is great; it is dreadful. Who can endure it? "Even now," declares the LORD, "return to me with all your heart, with fasting and weeping and mourning." Rend your heart and not your garments. Return to the LORD your God, for he is gracious and compassionate, slow to anger and abounding in love, and he relents from sending calamity. Who knows? He may turn and have pity and leave behind a blessing— grain offerings and drink offerings for the LORD your God. Blow the trumpet in Zion, declare a holy fast, call a sacred assembly. Gather the people, consecrate the assembly; bring together the elders, gather the children, those nursing at the breast. Let the bridegroom leave his room and the bride her chamber. Let the priests, who minister before the LORD, weep between the portico and the altar. Let them say, "Spare your people, O LORD. Do not make your inheritance an object of scorn, a byword among the nations. Why should they say among the peoples, 'Where is their God?'"

Joel 2:1-17

The Scriptures say that in the last days, God will be jealous for his people and will come down. He will deliver his people and restore to them what the locust has eaten. He will restore everything that has been lost and he will give us the former rain and the latter rain (Joel 2:23). He will pour out his Spirit on all flesh, with signs and wonders, with dreams and visions, for the great Day of the Lord is near (Joel 2:28).

His heart is burning with zeal, and the Father is saying that in this short time he wants to come down, to break the blindness, to break the captivity, to bring his Church out of slumber. The heart of God is intent on letting the Holy Spirit move over the earth one more time, through every person, through every people group, over all the earth, to break their bondage and set them free from their captivity. This is the zeal and the desire of God's heart.

The Heart and Purpose of God in This Hour
God began to speak to us about raising an army in early 2010. We heard the Spirit of God tell us to devote ourselves to building his

army. The more we prayed and sought him about this, the more we came to understand that God is not saying that we are the ones building his army; *God* is building his army all across the world. In every part of the world, on every continent, God is raising up a people who will stand as his soldiers. There are people everywhere that he is calling on to play one role or another in the raising of this army. Every time we have prayed about this, the Lord has said to us, "Remember, the army is not under your command. The army will be under the command of no man. It is my army, and I will command it."

One scripture he gave us in particular was Joel 2:11: "The LORD thunders at the head of his army; his forces are beyond number, and mighty are those who obey his command. The day of the LORD is great; it is dreadful. Who can endure it?"

Even without intention, our natural minds started to assume certain things concerning God's army. God had to fight with us to lay down these assumptions. We have since learned to tread softly, to be careful to not presume anything, to be careful to not touch his glory. The more we prayed into this, the more we realized that this revelation is sacred beyond our imagination. God is doing something that we have not seen in the past. And amazingly, as we have traveled around the world and shared with different people, we have met people who are hearing the same thing from God.

The deeper we and other people go in understanding what God is saying about this army, the more we tremble before the Lord and the more we realize that, although the Church of God has always been called the Army of God, God is raising an army – today – like none that has ever existed before. He said in the Scriptures that he is coming: "Blow the trumpet in Zion; sound the alarm on my holy hill. Let all who live in the land tremble, for the day of the LORD is coming. It is close at hand – a day of darkness and gloom, a day of clouds and blackness. Like dawn spreading across the mountains a large and mighty army comes, such as never was of old nor ever will be in ages to come" (Joel 2:1-2). This is a promise of God.

According to the Bible, just before the Day of the Lord comes, in the very last days, when evil, gloom, and clouds are hanging over the nations, there will be an army that will rise up. It will be a large and mighty army. It will be like dawn spreading across the mountains. It will be such as never was of old and never will be in ages to come. God put this in the Scriptures as a promise, and I believe that the days we are in right now are the days that the Lord said would come to pass.

We are the people who are living in this hour; therefore, we *are* the people of this destiny. This means that there are responsibilities we carry; there are requirements on our lives. And the time is short, the hour is late, the work is huge, the responsibilities are beyond comprehension.

So I want to ask you to pray for your own heart. "God Almighty, you created me and put me in this time in history for a purpose. I don't want to go another day without touching and gaining understanding about that purpose. You want and need to do something in my heart. I don't want to go on without that being fulfilled in me. God, speak to me. Speak to my heart like only you can and according to the way you know I'll be able to receive. Give me revelation. Give me wisdom. Give me understanding. Please give me the grace, the ability, and the revelation I need to be totally surrendered to you. Please answer me God, according to the way you've called me and anointed me. Let me do your work. Please set me apart and save me from sin, from my world's system, and from the works of the enemy so that your will and purposes can be fulfilled in my life. Amen."

Proclaim this among the nations: Prepare for war. Rouse the warriors! Let all the fighting men draw near and attack. Beat your plowshares into swords and your pruning hooks into spears. Let the weakling say, "I am strong!" Come quickly, all you nations from every side, and assemble there. Bring down your warriors, O Lord! Let the nations be roused; let them advance into the Valley of Jehoshaphat, for there I will sit to judge all the nations on every side. Swing the sickle, for the harvest is ripe. Come, trample the grapes, for the winepress is full and the vats overflow— so great is their wickedness! Multitudes, multitudes in the valley of decision! For the day of the Lord is near in the valley of decision.

Joel 3:9-14

God Is Calling for the Nations to Rise Up
The Lord is calling the nations to prepare for war. He is calling the nations to raise up their warriors, to raise up their fighting men and women, and to turn their working tools into fighting weapons. He is calling the nations everywhere to encourage even the weak among them to say they are strong in the Lord.

He is saying to the nations, "Come quickly! Come quickly all you nations; from every side." The hour is urgent. The need of the hour is great. What God is calling us to do is not something for us to sit and meditate about. This is something we must urgently rise up and do.

Then he says, "Bring down your warriors! Let the nations be roused." Roused! Let the nations be shaken out of their slumber. Let them be woken up! This is a direct call for action.

God's Army

God is raising up the army that he spoke of in Scripture. He is raising up that army to go and prepare the nations for what he is going to be doing, to prepare them for what is coming. This is an extraordinary time in which we live, and this is not just an ordinary army we are talking about. This is an army that has been foretold in Scriptures. This army has been spoken of by God.

Look at what Joel 2 says about this army. A large and mighty army comes such as has never been seen before and never will be seen again in the ages to come. This army goes before and devours things that are in its path. It leaves a fire behind as it goes by. This army has the appearance of horses, like a cavalry marching through the nations of the world. It leaps over the mountains and all the obstacles that stand in its way. It is being drawn up for battle.

At the sight of this army, the nations will anguish. Every face will turn pale. And the Scriptures say that it will charge forth like warriors that do not jostle one another; they all come into their calling and their position and their place. They begin to go forth under the orders of God, each having their own specific, God-given purpose and anointing.

The Lord foretold of this army. When you look at what was written in the Bible a millennium ago, and then you look at where we are today, you will realize that this army is *in our generation*. This army is being called forth and assembled *now*. I don't know how long it will take to raise up this army, but I know I'm being called to be a part of it. I know God is burdening me. "I *must* see a move of God!" It burns in my heart. We must see the nations rise up; we must see the nations move. I am being burdened to see the Church awakened, to see prayer spread like a fire across the nations.

We Are the Generation of the Prophesied Army

When you realize and understand that we are the generation of that army, that we are living in a day and time that was prophesied throughout the Scriptures, it gives implication to everything.

God has had a mission to accomplish through every generation that has come on this earth. He had a mission for Abraham. He had a mission for Moses and his generation, for Joshua and his generation, for the Apostles and their generation. And he has a mission our generation, and us; for the generation that exists in the last days, before that Last Day comes.

Jesus told the generation of his time that, "The generations will come and judge you because you did not fulfill the purpose that God had for this generation" (Luke 11:29-32). Now think of this: what burns in God's heart right now, in our generation? What burns in God's heart as he knows the beginning from the end? As we look at the state of the nations, the state of the Church, at what is coming, and see that time is growing later? What burns in God's heart? Is there any doubt? No.

We are a generation with a mandate to prepare the nations and ourselves for the Day of the Lord. The Bible speaks of our generation. It speaks of our time, the things we will face, and the things that we must prepare ourselves to do.

In the Bible there are different words for time. There is *chronos* time, which is chronological or sequential time, and there is *kairos* time, which are right or opportune moments. Kairos times are those defined moments when God is going to do something. Beloved, we live in a day, a transitional generation, in which God is going to do something in our time. Why are we seeing movements of transformation all over the world? Why are we seeing prayer being stirred and provoked all over the world? Why are people being called to lay everything down and surrender their lives so they can see God move in a mighty way?

What Kind of Vessels Do We Need to Be?

The Lord has said there are two things that are going to happen in this time in which we live. Joel 2:11 says that this season – this time – is going to be both great and terrible. There is a dual thing that is going to be happening during this time. Not only is there going to be a time and season of increased darkness, wickedness, and evil, but there is also going to be a great outpouring of his Holy Spirit. There is going to be a movement of God that has never before been seen on the face of the earth.

The prophet Haggai said that the glory of the latter house would be greater than the glory of the former house (Haggai 2:9). God said that he is going to work exploits, that he wants to prepare a Church that is victorious (Daniel 11:32). Not a church that is defeated, but a Church that rises up to its calling and its mission.

The Book of Acts displays the power of the Holy Spirit through that first-century Church. You see the way that the Church turned cities and nations upside down. But, beloved, the Bible tells us that the latter house in the last days will be even greater than that (Haggai 2:9). It talks about a power that will be released and a great movement of God that will move all over the world. God will raise up this army across the nations like a triumphant cavalry. He is going to be raising up a Church that is spotless and wrinkle-free (Ephesians 5:23). It will be a vessel he can use to create the greatest outpouring in the history of the world. No ministry will control it. It won't be led by a man or a woman; it will be led by the Lord himself.

What is provoked in you as we discuss this army that God is raising? It begins to make me want to cry out,

> *"Lord, if this is the time that you want to have your greatest outpouring, then what kind of vessel do I need to be? How do I need to give myself to you? If I live in the generation when you are raising up that kind of army, how do I need to live? How do I need to abandon my life? How purposeful do I need to be with my steps? How much do I need to abandon myself unto every word you speak to me? If the apostles had to submit and follow you, how much more do I need to be doing that right now? If this is the time that has been prophesied in your Word and you have placed us in that time, then how much more, Lord, do we need to abandon ourselves to you?"*

As we as individuals abandon ourselves to the Lord, depending on him to set us apart and make us into vessels he can use in these dark times, we will also see him do the same with today's Church. In these last days, a true Church will rise up. It will be powerful and mighty. It will be strong. It will not back away from suffering. It will be willing to die for the purposes of God, be willing to abandon everything to him. It will begin to be awakened with dreams and visions. It will begin to be burdened for the lost, hurting, and dying, like we have heard about revivals in times past. People will begin to rise up and believe God like never before, and God will begin to move and speak in great and mighty ways.

Beloved, this is the call of the hour. As the foundations crumble, we say "Yes" to our Lord. We say,

> "Yes, Lord, send me. Use me. Set me apart. Make me a vessel you can use. Make me a part of your army. Strengthen me and anoint me so I can stand against the darkness in these great and terrible days. I surrender to your will, Lord. I am yours and you are mine. Amen."

GROUP DISCUSSION QUESTIONS

General Discussion Questions (for whole group)

1. What is the general teaching we are seeking to grasp in this chapter?
2. What changes do we/you need to make in response to the lesson this week (in actions, mindset, etc)?
3. When you imagine the coming of God's army, what images come to mind?
4. What does it mean to be a member of the remnant? What does being a member of the remnant require of us?
5. Every member of God's army will have a role and a place. Why is it so critical that we understand our role in God's army? What might discourage or hinder our ability to know our role?
6. What will the Church of God look like as his army arises and comes into position? What will be the benefit of this army in the nations?

Personal Application Questions (for breakout groups)

1. What did the Lord impress upon your heart as you read this week?
2. "We are the people who are living in this hour; therefore, we are the people of this destiny." How do you feel about this statement?
3. What is provoked in you as we discuss this army that God is raising up?

4. How do we pray for one another as we rise up and take our position in the army of God?

Weekly Prayer Targets:
1. Ask the Lord to reveal how you are to ready yourself to be drafted into his army.
2. Pray for the enlargement and the consecration of the remnant from which this army will be called. Pray that the remnant will be large and that it will be strong.
3. Pray that the Lord will make you a vessel that he can use, and that he will strengthen you and make you able to stand against the darkness as you also cling to him and trust him to carry you through these days that are ahead.

Chapter 18

What Is Your Part in the Army of God?

This book was written with the hopes of awakening God people and helping them to see the "call of the hour." Our hearts are heavy with the Lord's burden of seeing the lost saved, nations awakened, individuals drawn into a deeper and eternal relationship with the Father, and the Lord's purposes fulfilled in and through our lives. We desire to see the Bride of Christ be awakened and prepared for the coming of the Day of the Lord, completing the mission he gave us to go disciple the nations.

We do not intend for this to be just another a good book that will be read and then placed on a shelf. No. Our desire is that this book would be a catalyst for you to begin to say, "Yes, Lord. What would you have me do?" And we trust the Lord to begin to do a work in you and through you so that – as part of the remnant that he is awakening in the nations – you can become part of the army that God is raising up all over the earth.

What God Is Doing in This Hour
The call to be set apart begins with an individual, but it transitions into a movement of God that will grow deeper in purity and holiness. Only God can do or will do this work, and as he does, more and more people will respond to his invitation to take part in what he is doing in our generation, and then be drawn into deeper levels of purity and holiness. We are going to see a reviving and refining fire of holiness in God's church as his people give themselves to this, and it will include all ages, races, ethnic groups, faith camps, cultures, and levels of society. God is going to be working this, and he will leave no one out, as he has said: ""every knee will bow before me; every tongue will confess to God" (Romans 14:11).

As we hear and respond to the call of God to be set apart, it will be necessary that we begin to allow him to work in and through us to prepare us for the work that he has for us to do. He will need to prepare our hearts and minds to be ready to take our place in the army that he is raising up. This can only be done through our full surrender to him and by placing our trust and faith in the covenant relationship he has offered to us.

As we walk deeper with the Lord, we will also begin to see that this work is not just on a personal level. Neither will it remain on a family, church, or local level. This is not something that is going to be between just you and God. No. It's going to increase. It's going to expand so that nations will recognize and acknowledge that there are people following the Lord. They are going to see Christians in a new light. They will begin to see that Christians are different; in the same way that God wanted to reveal himself through the nation of Israel, he is going to reveal himself to the nations through us.

The nations will see that there is real love in the Church and that this love is strong and powerful. This love is going to change nations. It's going to bring reconciliation where nothing else has worked. Where family counseling has failed, where human reasoning has failed, where political dialogue has failed. It's going to bring wars to an end, heal relationships, restore marriages, and draw the lost into the kingdom!

This movement of God will surpass anything that man can do. Many people around the world are sensing the Spirit of God saying that this is going to happen. Nations that have been at war are going to turn around as people submit themselves to the covenant love of God. As Christ's love is released, there will be reconciliation between people who have been enemies for years. Bondages and strategic rifts in territories that have been under darkness for ages are going to be broken as people in those areas give themselves to the Lord.

This is going to happen a great deal in the Middle East. We – the people of this generation – are going to see a blanket of darkness, hatred, and blindness be broken. The light will break forth, and whole populations are going to turn toward the Lord. The seeds of restoration have already started coming to fruition in nations like Algeria, Figi, and Saudi Arabia.

We are going to see an increase of this, but the fire – the embers of this fire – are going to be our surrendered and set apart lives. God is looking for a place where his presence can dwell, and when he finds a set apart life, that is the place from which he can move.

Those who surrender their lives to the Lord are going to be the forerunners, the ones who open the gates. They are going to be the ones who raise the banners, remove the stones so that the people can go forth (Isaiah 62:10).

Do not worry if for now you seem to be alone or if your group is small. You are already in the plan of God. You are already forerunners, opening spiritual gates that God is going to move through. You cannot know or imagine what God is going to be doing in the times to come.

As spiritual leaders and church leaders in a city with a burden and passion to be set apart for God, love God, and see his kingdom come and his purposes fulfilled begin to respond to this call, the Lord is going to begin to melt the divisions in the body of Christ and break the dividing walls. These leaders, the remnant, are going to find each other. They are going to speak and hear each other speaking in the same spirit, and an alliance is going to be created of men and women leaders in the same city. They are not going to allow themselves to be held back by anything denominational, cultural, or racial; they are going to come together with the burning love of Christ and a selfless surrender that will bring the churches in the city together.

Awakening in Cities
Those new to the set apart life may not be seeing this movement in their city right now, but begin to believe God for it. Begin to live for it. Trust the Lord that it is in his heart to do it. Trust that it will begin to happen. Pray for your leaders. Pray for the coming together of the churches.

For those pastors who have begun this walk, claim your pastor friends and other leaders in your church. Claim even those who may not be in your personal circle or network. Begin to believe that this is the next step of what God is going to do. It is going to melt the divisions of the churches in the city and he is going to raise up a body of Christ that knows no racial, social, cultural, or denominational boundaries or any other type of division.

People in your city will begin to come together in the unifying work of the Holy Spirit. As they do, there are going to be more powerful prayer gatherings. They might not necessarily be bigger gatherings, but prayer movements that will grow as leaders train and encourage their people to pray in their homes, workplaces, youth gatherings, and social gathering places, such as restaurants, playfields, shopping malls, etc. These times of prayer will grow and there will be more and more of them as God moves.

Prayer is going to become a common theme in the city. You will begin to see more and more prayer, especially among the young. We are going to see this as more and more young people begin to have a burning desire for God. Whoever you are and whatever you do, begin to encourage people to start to walk this journey.

As people begin to grow deeper in the Lord, they will begin to see bondages broken. Spiritual darkness will begin to be exposed; God is going to begin to open your eyes to things that have affected your family, that have been in your lineage, in your forefathers, and in your ancestry. God is going to begin to show you a connection of why things are in the natural, to show you the roots in the spirit. He will do this not only in families, but also in churches.

There are churches with dark backgrounds where things have happened in the past – church splits and sin – and been buried in the foundations. This darkness surfaces every now and then, destroying leaders, marriages, and relationships, so that churches are falling apart. This is so prevalent nowadays that sometimes we don't even see it; it has become what we consider normal in church life. But this is not what God intended for the Church, and he is raising up a standard to restore it.

As the darkness begins to be pushed back – strongholds are broken and people and the Church turn away from sin – whole communities and neighborhoods will be drawn together to hold solemn assemblies and cry to God, and God is promising to break these yokes of old, to bring healing and release. There is going to be exceeding joy as the Spirit of God brings freedom and forgiveness. And as whole communities will open up to the presence of God, the light of God will come into areas that have been covered in darkness.

There are inner cities in America and all around the world that have been in darkness a long time. Those who are living in these dark areas of crime, prostitution, addiction, drugs, and poverty will begin to seek God and to believe him for their salvation. As men and women in these areas begin to give themselves to the Lord, he is going to open their eyes and expose the darkness that has been hidden in their communities and the unholy covenants that have strengthened the grip of darkness. He is going to use his people in intercession and prayer to break the power of darkness over these areas and open the spiritual gates for his visitation.

There will be more and more church awakenings in cities where churches come together and have days of seeking days God. There will be prayer day and night, nights and evenings, and as the people pray, they will be set free. These awakenings won't be around big evangelists or huge crusades; they will occur on a more local basis around pastors who are burning for Christ, and will be because of a visitation from the Holy Spirit.

In the course of time, we are going to see city-wide awakenings; as men and women of God seek the Lord, whole cities are going to be opened up to his presence. We are going to see the prayer movement growing, not because it has been organized or been mobilized by some central place, but because people are being set apart, churches are being awakened, and people in the city are gathering in solemn assemblies.

This is going to spread across the world. We are going to hear more and more about the Spirit of God moving in this way in the nations, and we are going to see the Bride of Christ come alive and begin to be prepared for the Lord's coming. Praise God!

Give Yourself to the Lord, Who Is Our Only Hope

We are living in dark times and the hour is late. We cannot afford to turn aside and say, "I don't believe it." Neither can we allow the darkness to lull us into slumber, where we lose our zeal, our strength to repent, or our desire to see God's purposes fulfilled. We cannot say, "Let someone else do it," then sit in front of the TV.

People across the world are in need of awakening; they are in need of a Savior. Darkness and hopelessness have reigned for a long time. When the people are in such a needy and desperate state, for the sake of bringing them hope, we need to just step out, believe God, and say, "Lord, I want to see change in my area. I want you to use me, Lord, to see change in my people, in my generation."

These may be the last days, but the time of God's visitation is drawing near. So rise up. Cry out for him to move. Cross this line of surrendering your life to God, of asking him to set you apart. Begin to pray and seek the Lord and seek others of a like mind. Together, you are going to be forerunners he will use to open up the gates.

A Few Practical Steps to Begin the Journey of the Set Apart Life

We strongly believe that the first step toward successfully living the set apart life is prayer, both individually and corporately. The time you spend with God, both in prayer and in his Word, will strengthen you, feed you, and prepare you for the surrendered life. We therefore recommend that you begin to establish a daily prayer altar as well as begin to meet and pray with others on a regular basis.

Setting aside a daily time of prayer and being in the Word is a foundational element to the lifestyle of being surrendered to the Lord. It is in times of prayer that sin is exposed, healing takes place, insight is received, wisdom comes, and darkness is pushed back. You come to have a deeper and more intimate relationship with the Lord, and begin to trust and believe him in new and deeper ways.

Once your personal prayer altar has been established, begin to believe the Lord for a regular time of prayer with your family. The family prayer altar is also foundational to the walk and brings light into the home, as well as the protection, security, and provision we all need. The presence of the Lord is drawn into the home, and hearts begin to change. Relationships become stronger, parenting becomes easier, our children begin to come to Christ, and God begins to be glorified in our homes and our family.

For many of us, one of the first battles we face is for our family. With God's help, we can influence our family members and loved ones to come to the Lord. We can win the battle for their souls. Trust the Lord and pray. Don't believe the circumstances you see; believe God. Intercede for your family daily, like Job brought intercession for his children, in repentance and supplication. Wage warfare for each family member. Bring your loved ones to the altar; God will hear, and he answers prayer.

Also begin to seek out others and gather with them for prayer. Corporate prayer helps us grow deeper in prayer and intercession, and attracts the presence of the Lord as we seek him together. In corporate prayer, we can begin to hallow the name of the Lord, which releases fountains of worship and glorifies the Lord. God will begin to reveal what is happening around us, giving us insight into the spiritual realm. He will reveal things in the Spirit that we couldn't see before. He will reveal where he wants to take his people, and give them clear direction for what he wants them to do. This will encourage the people and give them hope for their families, their church, and their city. It will deepen our commitment to surrender and being used by God to establish his kingdom and fulfill his purposes.

Conclusion

I praise the Lord for what he is doing in this day and time, and I bless you as you begin or continue on your journey to be set apart for the Lord. *"Lord, I pray for those you have called into your work. Please give them the strength they need to give their whole hearts to you, to fully surrender their lives into your hands. Lord, may you be with them and guide them, and may your good and perfect will be done in and through their lives. We bless you, our Lord, and thank you for allowing us to join you in your redemptive work. It blesses us, Lord, to be among those you have called to be part of your army, and ask that every act, every thought, every word we speak be a blessing to your great name. Amen."*

GROUP DISCUSSION QUESTIONS

Discussion Questions (This week's questions will be for the whole group. Let this be a time of reflection as well as group celebration for what the Lord has revealed to all the members of your group and where he has taken each of you over the past weeks.)

1. What is the general teaching we are seeking to grasp in this chapter?
2. What changes do we/you need to make in response to the lesson this week (in actions, mindset, etc)?
3. What did the Lord impress upon your heart as you read this week?
4. What has the Lord laid on your heart as the next step to take in your Nazirite walk?
5. What has been the most significant life change that has happened to you through the course of this study?

6. List three things you are grateful for that came through this study. If time allows, explain.
7. Spend the remainder of your group time praising the Lord for all that he has done through this study.

Weekly Prayer Targets:

1. Ask the Lord to fully awaken you and set you apart so that you can be a vessel he can use in these last days.
2. Spend time this week seeking the Lord for direction and revelation regarding
   a. Your role in God's army
   b. The next step in your Nazirite walk
   Be prepared to share what the Lord reveals during your group study time.
3. Ask the Lord to continue to take you deeper into surrender and the set apart lifestyle, as well as continue to teach you how to pray into and maintain your covenant position with him.

Our Ministry
World Trumpet Mission is a catalyst for revival in the nations. We have been called by the Lord to "blow" the trumpet, awaken the Bride of Christ, and prepare the people of God for the coming Day of the Lord.

We are an interdenominational, international missionary organization that sends missionaries into the nations of the world to seek transforming revival by drawing the presence of the Lord through prayer, repentance, praise and worship, and a lifestyle surrendered to being set apart to God.

The goal of our missionaries is to awaken the Church in an area and together with the city Church, to seek city-wide awakening through unity, deepening of prayer, a lifestyle of praise and worship, and pushing back the darkness until a breakthrough comes through which the kingdom of God becomes manifest.

Our Mission
Our mission is to awaken, equip, and provoke the people in the city to be able to carry on the tranforming work of God in their lives, homes, churches, cities, and nations.

To Support Our Mission
If you are interested in supporting the missions work of World Trumpet Mission, you may send donations to the address below, call our office at (407)846-8300, email office@worldtrumpet.com, or make donations directly on our website at www.worldtrumpet.com

To Contact Us
For further information about the mission and vision of World Trumpet Mission, please visit our website: www.worldtrumpet.com.

You may also write or call us at:

World Trumpet Mission-US
PO Box 770447
Orlando, FL 32877
USA
Tel: (407)846-8300
Email: office@worldtrumpet.com

You may also be interested in the following messages from
Pastor John Mulinde and Pastor Mark Daniel:

Covenant
DVD/CD/MP3 $25/$20/$15

Covenant forms the basis of Christianity, the bedrock on which our faith is built. Exploring both the Old and New Testament, Pastors John Mulinde and Mark Daniel powerfully address the historical and practical elements of covenant, the nature of the covenant God made with man, and the implications of the covenant for us in these days. This series of three teachings will broaden your understanding and faith.

Raising the Level of Prayer
CD/MP3 $20/$15

Communion with God is the essence of prayer. It is through prayer that we come into a deeper and more intimate relationship with our Father, his Son, and his Holy Spirit. Not only does prayer lead us to a dynamic and intensifying relationship with Christ, it also leads us to levels of trust, faith, spiritual insight, and intercession we would not reach without spending time in the presence of the Lord.

In this series of four teachings, Pastor Mark Daniel speaks on the foundational truths of asking, seeking, and knocking, and of earnestly seeking God with no pretense. He also shares the importance of developing a lifestyle of prayer and praise, and saturating ourselves – our minds and souls – in the Word of God.

This series will bless those who desire to strengthen their prayer life, and thus their relationship with God.

Discovering the Power of the Holy Spirit
CD/MP3 $15/$10

We have received incomparable power through the gift of the Holy Spirit, yet we struggle to live in the reality of the deep communion and ongoing flow of life found in him. Many Christians are frustrated at their obvious lack of power, knowing that there is much more to the Christian life, but not knowing how to touch it.

In this three-part series, Pastor Mark Daniel shares several keys to how to tap into the power of the Holy Spirit, how we can be led by the Spirit, and how we can give him control of our lives as we learn to live dependant on God.